Personal Effectiveness

Guiding People
to Assert Themselves
and Improve
Their Social Skills

Robert Paul Liberman
Larry W. King
William J. DeRisi
Michael McCann

Research Press
2612 North Mattis Avenue
Champaign, Illinois 61820

ISBN 0-87822-163-8

The work which led to this Guide was supported in part by Research Grant MH 26207-01 from the Mental Health Services Research and Development Branch of the National Institute of Mental Health.

Illustrated by Libby Hayes, UCLA Media Center

This book is dedicated to the creative, enthusiastic, and skill-ful clinicians of the Oxnard Regional Mental Health Center whose fine personal qualities have blended with principles of learning to make the techniques described here effective and helpful with thousands of individuals who have learned to express their feelings and improve their social skills.

Contents

Foreword

This guide to Personal Effectiveness training is useful to the helping professional who accepts the challenge of the great number of persons needing enlargement and refinement of their social and emotional skills. For many such persons, traditional insight-oriented psychotherapy, individual or group, is ineffective; too expensive; available with great difficulty; or strikingly limited when verbal skills, education, or psychological-mindedness are limited.

During the 1960's a variety of new therapies flourished that attempted to supply what the earlier insight-oriented therapies did not. These therapies include Transactional Analysis, Gestalt Therapy, Behavior Therapy, Encounter Groups, and Family Therapy. Personal Effectiveness belongs in this list. As a broad-spectrum, behavioral therapy, it is concerned with both the altered quality of an individual's behavior and the effect of that behavior on his social world. It is used best by professionals who have experience in the assessment of clinical problems and some background in behavior therapy, who are comfortable with an active, specific, and operational clinical style. This book provides, for such professionals, step-by-step detail about actual use of the procedures that constitute Personal Effectiveness. It also offers self-testing feedback opportunities and experiential practice exercises designed to further enhance learning and measure mastery of the procedures. Less experienced professionals, in groups or as a working staff, can use this basic manual together with the accompanying *Program Guide, Client's Introduction,* and *demonstration film* for learning the procedures as part of continuing education.

The main procedures in Personal Effectiveness have been used by other clinicians with similar goals. The procedures include social modeling, prompting and instructions, behavioral practice and rehearsal, reinforcement, discrimination and shaping. All are supported by sound research of the past 10-20 years. Assertion Training and Social Skills Training use the same procedures but have narrower goals. Structured Learning Therapy comes closest to Personal Effectiveness but does not deal with as great a range of emotional and interpersonal expressiveness problems presented by all social classes.

Personal Effectiveness rests upon the translation of complex, often mysterious, social and emotional processes into concretely meaningful steps and tools for use in daily life. A major and comforting difference between Personal Effectiveness and almost all other recent innovative therapies is the emphasis upon research underlying the principles and procedures used, and upon documentation of the learner's progress by a number of means. The Annotated Bibliography summarizes relevant, scientific inquiries, while the sample record keeping forms provide a means of conveniently and meaningfully documenting client progress. Numerous examples clarify the sequence of Personal Effectiveness sessions, carefully detailing the Planning Meeting—Training Session—Evaluation Meeting sequence.

The wide range of people with whom Personal Effectiveness procedures have proved useful include students, children, parents, married couples, management trainees, mental health trainees, corrections officers, and psychotic and neurotic patients. The problems for which these procedures have been useful include workshops in marriage counseling, crisis interventions, anxiety, depression, child rearing, peer relationships at various ages, consumerism, transportation, and recreation.

A recent development, probably a consequence of the wide utility of these procedures in the hands of experienced clinicians, is the increasing combined use of Personal Effectiveness with long-term, insight-oriented, individual psychotherapy. For example, psychoanalytically based therapy can be used with Personal Effectiveness either by one clinician or by a clinician and a consultant, with either procedure being initial or subsequent.

A feature which highly commends this book is the spirit implied in the last paragraph of the authors' Introduction. "We solicit the positive and negative reactions to our book by all readers since we plan to update and improve it periodically. We are particularly eager to obtain the benefit of the counselors' experiences when attempting to use Personal Effectiveness in their work in order to establish more specific uses and limitations of this approach." Personal Effectiveness procedures do not pretend to solve all of a person's problems, nor even necessarily to solve those identified as appropriate to the method, with complete accuracy. Rather, Personal Effectiveness helps a person to recognize that he can exert influence in shaping his own life and can do so without injustice to others and without the consequence of social isolation. How refreshingly in the Darwinian spirit is the authors' solicitation of "the positive *and* the negative reactions of *all* readers," by comparison with the grandiose, undocumented assertions of so many promoters of new therapies!

George Saslow, M.D.
Professor of Psychiatry
UCLA School of Medicine

Acknowledgments

This manual is a distillation of four years experience in developing and evaluating methods for training people in social and emotional skills at the Oxnard Mental Health Center and Camarillo State Hospital, Oxnard, California. The dedicated efforts of the mental health professionals at the Oxnard Mental Health Center and the Clinical Research Unit of Camarillo State Hospital have made these efforts fruitful and worth disseminating more widely. The following clinicians have used Personal Effectiveness to help over 1000 clients achieve greater interpersonal competence and satisfaction: Johnie Roberts, R.N., Nancy Sanders, R.N., Gayle McDowell, R.N., Charlotte Hoffer, R.N., Edwin Bryan, Jr., M.H.T., Dennis Cain, M.H.T., Frank Dell, M.H.T., James Bedwell, M.H.T., Emilio Flores, M.H.T., Richard Gonzalez, M.H.A., Ramon Rocha, M.S.W., Eugenie Wheeler, M.S.W., Wayne Rimmer, M.S.W., Louis de Visser, Ph.D., Ann Hanson, M.S.W., Vikki Smith, M.H.T., James Teigen, M.S.W., John Davis, B.A., Charles Wallace, Ph.D., Sandra Lenhardt, B.A., Larry Licker, M.S.W., Lalo Perez, M.S.W., Robert Soliz, M.S.W., and Nancy Austin, B.A.

The authors are grateful for the support and encouragement of Drs. Rafael Canton, Sarah Miller, and Stephen Coray, Administrative Directors of the Ventura County Mental Health Department and Health Services Agency.

We also wish to thank James Teigen and Impact Press for their permission to use the material in Table 1, and S. A. Rathus and *Behavior Therapy* for their permission to use the "30-item schedule for assessing assertive behavior."

Introduction

In our society there are schools and educational opportunities for almost every conceivable human skill, from scuba diving and dancing to dentistry and computer programming. Systematic training and apprenticeships are available for people who want to learn anything from carpentry to surgery. For those people who do not have social and emotional skills, however, there is a void of remedial opportunities. While psychotherapy, individual and group, is aimed at helping people integrate their personalities, improve their relationships, and function at higher levels, it is not consistently effective, freely and inexpensively available, nor suitable for those with little education or verbal skills. Now, however, Personal Effectiveness, a broad-spectrum behavioral therapy, is available to teach people from varied walks of life a wide range of emotionally expressive and social skills.

The learning principles which have been drawn together to form the procedures inherent in Personal Effectiveness—social modeling, prompting, reinforcement, discrimination, behavioral practice, rehearsal, and shaping—have been arrayed in similar ways by other clinicians and termed Assertion Training, Emotional Training, Social Skills Training, and Structured Learning Therapy. We call our procedure Personal Effectiveness because we view the methods as relevant and applicable for all types of emotional and interpersonal expressiveness, and because we feel that the best indicator of successful outcome of this type of therapy is not just the improved quality of the client's behavior, but also the *effect* that this behavior has on his social life.

This manual has been written for all disciplines within the helping professions to provide a guide, or "how-to-do-it," experience for those who want to master Personal Effectiveness. The procedures are valuable to psychology, psychiatry, social work, counseling, guidance, nursing, rehabilitation, corrections, education, and personnel and employee development. No special professional training is necessary for grasping and gaining competence as a trainer in Personal Effectiveness, although the counselor should possess basic human skills such as warmth, empathy, sensitivity, and a ready ability to express all forms of emotions before beginning a course in Personal Effectiveness. A psychiatric technician or aide, given these basic human emotional skills, can use Personal Effectiveness as well as a highly trained psychiatrist or clinical psychologist. The methods described in this manual will be learned and applied more rapidly by those with previous experience in the helping professions, and by those who are comfortable with an active, specific, and operational style of working with clients or students.

People who can make use of this book are listed below:

1. Practicing mental health clinicians, such as psychiatrists, psychologists, social workers, nurses, aides, technicians, occupational and recreational therapists, and rehabilitation counselors.

2. Pastors and other clergy who are called upon to assist their parishioners with personal problems.

3. General practitioners and other physicians who treat large numbers of patients with "functional" or psychosomatic disorders.

4. Psychotherapists who are curious and interested in adding a new and effective technique to their clinical repertoires.

5. Teachers and school counselors who want to find new approaches for improving classroom behavior, teacher-student relationships, and peer relationships among students.

6. Personnel officers and others in governmental agencies, executive offices, industries, and business who wish to improve morale and productivity of their workers and establish optimum employer-employee working relationships.

7. Interested lay people and parents who would like to improve their relationships with their children, friends, and relatives.

Although Personal Effectiveness procedures can be used in individual or group sessions, efficiency and clinical experience indicate that a more extensive use of the group format is preferable. Personal Effectiveness groups are highly structured and goal oriented; also a large number of clients can receive training in a short period of time. Each Personal Effectiveness session consists of a Planning Meeting, a Training Session, and an Evaluation Meeting.

The prime objective of the Planning Meeting is to enable each group member to choose a behavioral goal for the training session. The goal involves a *feeling* or *action* to practice with another person in a role playing scene. During the Planning Meeting clients also report back to the group members and leaders on their completion of "homework" assignments from the previous session. Successful completion of an assignment provides an opportunity for the leader and other group members to praise the client's performance. Strong group cohesion is developed through demonstrations of success, mutual support, and positive feedback.

The Training Session consists of each client role playing the person-to-person situation or scene he selected during the Planning Session. The group leader directs the scenes and uses himself, co-leaders or other clients. Typical scenes that are role played are talking with a spouse, "leveling" with a parent or teacher, being firm with subordinates, asking for a job application, asking for a date, expressing affection to a loved one, initiating a conversation with a stranger, expressing anger or annoyance directly without being insulting, accusative, or aggressive, and calling a friend or neighbor to arrange a social visit. Specific feedback is given to each client on his performance during the role playing. Eye contact, posture, gestures, facial expression, voice quality, and content and fluency of speech are components of communication that receive attention. The counselor emphasizes positive feedback and encourages small progressive steps. Following the role play and feedback, the group leader may call on a coleader or another client to demonstrate or model how they would improve one or two of these components. The client then enacts the role play a second time and is rewarded by the group for improvements in performance. A specific assignment, such as "Ask the manager of the store for a job application," or "Ask the woman at school to have coffee with you" is written on a small card and given to each client. Clients are encouraged to complete the assignment and to report back at the next group meeting. When each client in the group has role played a behavioral goal and received an assignment, the Training Session ends.

The Evaluation Meeting offers an opportunity for group leaders to receive feedback from one another and from clients who are invited to attend the meeting. One purpose of the meeting is to let the leaders know how others viewed their performance. As in the Training Sessions, the emphasis during evaluation is on positive feedback; for example, "Johnnie, that was a beautiful job of modeling the use of hands and posture for Betty." A second purpose is to troubleshoot difficulties in the group. The manual is oriented primarily toward giving the reader a practical understanding of Personal Effectiveness. Additional components to be used in conjunction with the manual are a Personal Effectiveness *Program Guide,* which provides the group leader with supplementary information for practice exercises and questions in this manual; it also coordinates this manual with a Personal Effectiveness *demonstration film.* These components aid an entire staff of a facility to obtain more direct and experiential learning of the methods. It is helpful to use the book in a coordinated way while applying the methods directly with clients and students. However, for those with little background in behavior therapy, further supervision and training beyond the manual are recommended for gaining competence and mastery as a trainer in Personal Effectiveness. There is also a short pamphlet, the *Client's Introduction*, which orients clients' expectations toward a Personal Effectiveness session.*

At the Oxnard (California) Community Mental Health Center, Personal Effectiveness procedures have been used in the outpatient clinic, the day hospital, and in public education and community consultation. Group leaders have incorporated Personal Effectiveness into marriage counseling, training parents in child management, anxiety and depression management groups, groups for children, adolescents, and young adults, and crisis intervention groups. In the day hospital, an educational model of treatment is used in which clients attend workshops dealing with problems in living. In workshops such as consumerism, personal finance, use of public agencies, grooming, recreation, and transportation, Personal Effectiveness methods help clients learn how to have more active and satisfying lives in their community. Training in Personal Effectiveness, also called Assertion Training, has been successfully used with women's consciousness-raising groups, management development programs, probation officers, and as a means for teaching counseling skills to mental health professionals and paraprofessionals. These are only a sample of the range of possible applications of Personal Effectiveness. With an understanding of the principles of Personal Effectiveness provided by this manual, the counselor can use his own creativity and ingenuity to apply the procedures to his own particular areas of interest. Personal Effectiveness will enhance the skills of both the counselor and clients alike.

The format for Personal Effectiveness was developed by Robert Liberman beginning in 1970 and was applied by the clinical staff of the Oxnard Mental Health Center for a wide range of problems presented by outpatients and day-care

* R. P. Liberman, L. W. King, W. J. DeRisi and Michael McCann. *Personal Effectiveness: Guiding people to assert themselves and improve their social skills. Program Guide; Demonstration film; Client's introduction.* Champaign, ILL.: Research Press, 1975.

patients. The procedures were refined and systematized by Robert Liberman, Larry King, and William DeRisi during the 1972-74 period when a research grant from the National Institute of Mental Health enabled a project team to engage in program development and evaluation at the Oxnard Center. During 1973-74, Larry King applied Personal Effectiveness in a large scale management development program sponsored by the U.S. Navy; he also carried out evaluative and experimental research on the outcomes of training in Personal Effectiveness. DeRisi and Liberman applied the methods with outpatient groups of married couples and with people complaining of anxiety and depression. Michael McCann's literary talents led to a rough draft of the book which was put into final form by Liberman with editorial inputs from King and DeRisi.

The world is full of people who lack Personal Effectiveness. Whether their problems surface in a mental hospital, a counseling clinic, a classroom, or a business office, unassertive people have difficulty meeting their social and material needs. They are often exploited, pushed aside, or simply ignored in the bustle of everyday life. Rather than taking an *active* part in their environments, they are *acted upon* by others. Where and how can people learn the social and communication skills needed for Personal Effectiveness? Counselors, therapists, educators, rehabilitation workers, personnel managers, and organizers need practical and workable methods to help teach people to express their feelings and obtain their needs effectively.

We are sensitive to the ethical and professional hazards of offering a new technique for general use. We would not recommend that others use a method that has not been empirically and adequately evaluated and researched. Ten years of experimental research and program evaluations of the package of behavioral learning techniques included in Personal Effectiveness have clearly documented its effectiveness with a wide variety of clinical problems in the hands of large numbers of therapists in many different settings. This body of research is referenced in the Annotated Bibliography at the end of the book. We have chosen to refer readers to the voluminous literature rather than trying to summarize it here in order to avoid diluting the practical and clinical focus of the manual.

We solicit the positive and negative reactions to our book by all readers since we plan to update and improve it periodically. We are particularly eager to obtain the benefit of the counselor's experiences when attempting to use Personal Effectiveness in their work in order to establish more specific uses and limitations of this approach.

Chapter 1
Background and Procedures

Personal Effectiveness is Communication

The personal problems that people have every day frequently stem from their inability to express their feelings or to communicate their interests and desires to others who are important to them. Person-to-person communication is one of the most essential of our uniquely human capacities. Each day we must satisfy our emotional, social, and biological needs by interacting effectively with other people—with our families at home, with employers and co-workers on the job, with clerks and officials in government and the marketplace, with friends and relatives at play and in social situations. When we are unable to get our feelings across to others or to meet our needs, our quality of life is diminished. When we are shut off from expressing our feelings or from having satisfying relationships with other people, we are stunted and stifled and pay the price with limited pleasures, depression, loneliness, anxiety, and psychosomatic ills.

Improvements in our social skills allow us to more effectively pursue our interests, exploit opportunities, and to live more emotionally rewarding lives. Successes in our social life shape more effective communication skills. The availability and visibility of parents, siblings, friends, and media heroes as appropriate models help us acquire expressive competency through the process of imitation or identification. The naturally rewarding consequences of effective communication, such as friendships and social approval, are usually sufficient to strengthen and broaden our range of appropriate emotional behaviors. Because this is a normal developmental

1

process we are often unaware of the fact that we have learned a complex behavioral repertoire. We may only be aware of the learning processes involved when we confront novel or difficult situations that require new social and emotional responses from us. For example, we might become conscious of our assets and limitations in social communication if we were going to be introduced to a member of British royalty, had an interview lined up for an important job, were called upon to speak at a banquet, or had to tell someone about the death of someone close to him. To prepare for a challenging and new social situation, you would probably rehearse to yourself, or possibly practice in front of others. You might seek out other people who were doing these things, watch them in action, and note how they carried out these activities so that you could do them in a similar way. Personal Effectiveness attempts to teach assertiveness by using similar techniques.

There are two reasons why people have problems expressing feelings such as friendship and affection; annoyance and anger; joy and pleasure; sadness and grief; interest and concern for others; and self-assertiveness and confidence. Some people have never learned to express these emotions because they have not had the good fortune to be exposed to appropriate models while growing up with their families or among their friends. This lack of exposure and hence learning opportunities with good role models may often be compounded by biological deficiencies. The other primary cause of problems in emotional and social expressiveness comes from environmental stress, personal traumas and losses, or sudden changes in one's social world—situational events that evoke anxiety or depression which, in turn, interfere with and inhibit one's spontaneity and emotional and interpersonal expressiveness.

When problems of too little expression of feelings—such as social isolation; or a too high intensity of expressiveness—such as aggression and persistent elation, mount over a period of time, the affected individual or his concerned family members often seek help from human service agencies. Psychiatric hospitals, mental health centers, counseling

2

centers, family service agencies, personnel offices, police, and the consulting rooms of physicians and clergymen are filled with people whose problems lie in deficiencies or excesses of social and emotional expression. For example, consider the predicaments of the following people who have sought assistance at a community mental health center:

Jerry, an 8-year-old boy, has no friends.

He is shy and withdrawn with peers and talks only to adults.

Mary, at age 15, has been suspended from school for fighting.

She is belligerent with peers as well as authority figures and pushed a teacher who criticized her. She has not distinguished between aggressiveness and assertiveness.

John, a dedicated and competent architect, has been passed over for three promotions and is depressed.

He works productively and efficiently, but speaks in a monotone and averts his gaze from people when talking to them.

Matthew has marriage problems.

He isn't able to tell his wife, in a positive way, what he wants from her and is awkward expressing tenderness.

Jane has dating problems.

She feels uptight with men and "freezes" without knowing how to respond to conversation and affection.

Tim is introverted and lonely.

He has trouble starting conversations with strangers.

Pat can't get a job.

She rarely smiles and speaks so low that others have difficulty hearing her.

Arthur annoys people and has spent time in jail.

He can't distinguish aggressiveness from assertiveness and deals with people in an insolent and abrasive manner.

These people can be helped to deal with life's challenges if they can learn to communicate more effectively. One component of person-to-person communication is the verbal or semantic content of speech. Our choice of words and putting them together into sentences and phrases gives meaning to our interactions with others. But even more important for conveying meaning is the manner or the way we say our

Matthew avoids looking
at his wife when speaking to her

words and phrases. *How* we talk and communicate is perhaps more important than *what* we say. Choosing our words carefully may make us more articulate, but our nonverbal style of interacting more impressionistically, intuitively, and spontaneously engenders judgments, evaluations, and reactions from others. Facial expression, gestures, eye contact, posture, sighs, laughs, tone and loudness of voice, and fluency and pacing of speech are essential nonverbal behaviors in communication. These nonverbal components of social behavior are the media which carry a large part of our meanings and, in turn, our messages.

Table 1, page 6 presents a summary of the distinctions among self-assertiveness, passivity, and aggressiveness. Since the meaning of behavior varies from situation to situation, there are no absolute and clear dividing lines between reasonable and appropriate assertiveness, aggression or passivity. Thus many people go to one extreme (aggression) or the other (passivity).

The Counselor's Role

Social and emotional communication can be taught to people who lack effective verbal and nonverbal skills. When helping people to reach out for human contact and to express their feelings, the same principles of learning that are used in teaching any other skill are used. The counselor:

1. Breaks the required behaviors into specific, concrete, small steps or building blocks.

2. Gives clear instructions and prompts for the desired behavior, repeating them as he guides the trainee through a rehearsal.

3. Encourages the person to practice, in small steps, under his direct supervision.

4. Exposes the person to role models who can demonstrate more effective ways of communicating.

5. Gives positive and negative feedback, shaping the person gradually, step-by-step into better ways of communicating.

Table 1 How Assertiveness Differs from Passivity and Aggressiveness on Behavioral Dimensions

PASSIVE PERSON	ASSERTIVE PERSON	AGGRESSIVE PERSON
Has Rights Violated; Is Taken Advantage Of	Protects Own Rights and Respects the Rights of Others	Violates Rights; Takes Advantage of Others
Does Not Achieve Goals	Achieves Goals Without Hurting Others	May Achieve Goals at Expense of Others
Feels Frustrated, Unhappy Hurt, and Anxious	Feels Good About Self; Has Appropriate Confidence in Self	Defensive, Belligerent; Humiliates and Depreciates Others
Inhibited and Withdrawn	Socially and Emotionally Expressive	Explosive; Unpredictably Hostile and Angry
Allows Others to Choose for Him	Chooses for Self	Intrudes on Others' Choices

Adapted by James Teigen from *Your Perfect Right* by R. E. Alberti and M. L. Emmons. San Luis Obispo, CA.: Impact Press, 1974.

6. Provides explicit "homework" assignments for graded practice, in real life, between training sessions.

7. Rewards successful approximations of the desired behaviors with approval and praise.

Historical Development of Personal Effectiveness

Methods for teaching people to improve their social and emotional responsiveness became systematic and well-defined with the work of Andrew Salter twenty-five years ago. In 1949, Salter's *Conditioned Reflex Therapy* was published; it describes methods for facilitating the self-expression of neurotic patients to help them overcome anxiety, depression, and other maladaptive traits. Wolpe, in his 1958 pioneering work, *Psychotherapy by Reciprocal Inhibition,* pointed out that patients could master their fears by learning assertive responses since a person who is expressing his feelings with vigor cannot at the same time feel anxious. Lazarus (1966) used the term "behavioral rehearsal" for a combination of modeling and role playing aimed at increasing patients' assertiveness. Wolpe, Salter, Lazarus and others have used the term Assertion or Assertive Training when describing an approach for helping someone acquire or reestablish appropriate emotional expressiveness. People who can benefit from Assertion Training may never have learned how to show anger, or may have been punished or ignored while asserting their feelings (often in childhood) and hence have learned to have anxious and passive responses to interpersonal situations.

Assertive behavior enables a person to act in his own best interests, to stand up for himself without undue anxiety, and to exercise his rights without denying the rights of others (Alberti and Emmons, 1974). The assertive individual defends his own rights and respects the rights of others, in contrast with the passive individual whose rights are violated and who is taken advantage of, or the aggressive individual who violates others' rights and takes advantage of others. The assertive person takes an active part in his work and social life; he chooses and achieves his goals, but not at the expense of others. Therapists and counselors may incorrectly assume that their clients must certainly *know* how to express their positive and negative emotions and need only to understand *why* they fail in self-expression. This is often a false assumption leading to frustrating and unsuccessful experiences for both the client and the therapist. Many people simply do not have the appropriate self-assertive responses in their repertoires, and they need to be taught and shown directly and concretely *how* to express their feelings through demonstrations of words and actions.

During the 1960's, applications of Skinner's research in operant conditioning led to a broader view of helping people who were deficient in their emotional and social communication. The focus for remedial work was expanded beyond neurotics to retardates, delinquents, psychotics in institutions, and then to working systematically in therapy groups (for reviews of this work see Liberman, 1972(a); Rimm and Masters, 1974). Emotions, in addition to self-assertiveness and standing up for one's rights, were operationalized and targeted for change—joy, cohesiveness, conversational skills, rational talk (with delusional schizophrenics), affection, tenderness, and sadness. Bandura's research in social learning led to the incorporation of modeling procedures into Assertion Training (Bandura, 1969). Bandura and other behaviorists have clearly demonstrated how a range of emotions, from rage and aggression to tenderness and love, can be learned by one person observing and imitating a model. The content of speech, gestures, facial expressions, vocal tone and pace, and body movements combine to communicate feelings; each of these components can be learned by observing relevant models. For example, research has shown that people rated high in assertiveness speak longer in response to questions, talk louder, request more frequent changes in their environment, and pause for shorter periods than do those who are perceived to be unassertive. Assertion Training is a successful method for helping people overcome a large variety of problems. Examples are given below.

Problem	*Goals of Assertion Training*
Violent aggression	To express frustration and anger in words and to obtain social

	and material needs through appropriately firm and persistent requests.
Fears and phobias in social situations	To practice speaking up in gradually larger gatherings of groups of people.
Impotence and pedophilia	To be assertively expressive with women.
Marital discord	To express feelings directly and spontaneously with spouse. To give pleasing, positive remarks to spouse and to express negative feelings without being accusative.
Suicidal behavior	To obtain concern and interest from others using words and nonverbal components of self-expression.

At the Oxnard (California) Community Mental Health Center and the Camarillo-Neuropsychiatric Institute Research Center (UCLA), a broadened and more comprehensive form of Assertion Training has been developed. In 1970, Robert Liberman and his colleagues evolved a practical framework for teaching emotional expression and social skills in groups. Over half the goals of clients who have participated in these groups have focused on conversational and social approach behaviors. For example, clients are taught to initiate conversations with relatives, friends, and strangers and are given instructions about how to maintain and terminate conversations once they are begun. The rudiments of effective conversational skills are practiced—such as eye contact, adequate voice volume and intonation, proper pacing and fluency of speech, and demonstrative use of gestures and facial expressions. Some clients work on initiating new relationships, as in dating. An important component of sustained human interaction is giving and asking for information and opinions; this skill is taught systematically to those who are shy, withdrawn or who complain by saying, "I don't ever know what to say." Preparing for job interviews, an important survival skill in community adjustment, is another major goal of training in Personal Effectiveness. Learning how to give and accept criticism and praise is the focus for about 10 percent of the Personal Effectiveness goals. However, using the conventional meanings of assertiveness, only about 15 percent of rehearsed situations deal with standing up for one's rights.

Examples of clients and the problems that responded favorably to Personal Effectiveness at the community mental health center are given below:

A college student who was unable to make friends

A man who was nagged by his wife

A middle-aged woman who was afraid to ask her landlord to make repairs

An attractive girl in her early twenties who was unable to express her emotions in conversations

A man who was unable to stand up to his boss' unfair criticism

A drug abuser who was unable to express himself, to reject overtures to use drugs, and who seemed disinterested in other people

A 30-year old man who avoided all social contact

A 46-year-old wife and mother who couldn't set limits with her adolescent son, and who was reluctant to tell her husband that she wanted to return to work

A 33-year-old foreman in a factory who had great difficulty confronting his employees with their poor performances, and who was developing anxiety at work

A 29-year-old woman who was chronically depressed, and who expressed resentment to her husband by sulking

A mother of four children who felt overburdened by child-rearing responsibilities, but who was afraid to ask her husband for help in disciplining and managing their children.

A basic assumption of structured learning approaches to emotional expression, supported by research evidence, is that acquiring the outward manifestations or signs appropriate to

A depressed wife who expresses
resentment to her husband
by sulking

an emotion is subsequently followed by the inner or subjective experience of that feeling. For instance, after several sessions of practicing the postural, gestural, vocal, and facial expressions consonant with tenderness and affection to his wife, a husband, who initially claimed to have little feelings of affection for her, will describe the gradual return of warmth, pleasure, and internal comfort. Furthermore, concentrating on the teachable and demonstrable outward signs of affection is a more efficient, faster means for bringing about emotional change than is a direct focus on the inner feelings in therapeutic discussion and interaction. Experiencing the inner, subjective, and physiological qualities of joy, pleasure, anger, assertiveness, tenderness, and affection is promoted by direct practice and rehearsal of the external behavioral signs of these feelings and by the favorable reactions that clear and direct behavioral expressions engender in others. Practitioners of Personal Effectiveness assume that changes in self-esteem, self-confidence, attitudes, and subjective discomfort follow rather than precede changes in overt behavior. Based on this assumption, the emphasis in Personal Effectiveness is on first helping the client to change his or her behavior in visible and audible ways. The clients, trainees, and students participating in Personal Effectiveness will feel better about themselves after seeing and hearing themselves behaving effectively and getting positive results in their material and social worlds.

Training Procedures in Personal Effectiveness

Personal Effectiveness is carried out in groups of 4-15 clients or students with two professional or paraprofessional leaders. Individual sessions between one client and a therapist or counselor can also be used alone or as a supplement to group sessions. Personal Effectiveness groups are generally composed of people with a variety of different problems and goals as well as with people sharing similar characteristics, problems, and goals. At the Oxnard Community Mental Health Center, weekly outpatient groups meet separately. There is a group for those people coping with marital problems, those suffering anxiety and depression, those with child-parent conflicts, and another for situational crises. The Personal Effectiveness groups in the Day Treatment Center, where clients come daily for one to three months as an alternative to, or transition from, hospitalization, are heterogeneously composed of those with many different problems in living. The patients in the Day Treatment Center suffer from severe depression, schizophrenia, manic-depression, suicidal preoccupations, and extreme situational disturbances that have impaired social and role functioning. The Day Treatment Center, operating with an intensive, educational approach, offers Personal Effectiveness groups four days each week. More frequent practice and training sessions are necessary for more severely impaired clients and the closely spaced group sessions facilitate rapid acquisition and learning of the social and emotional skills that are necessary for community adjustment. Even *overlearning*, repeated practice beyond the point of the first few successes with interpersonal behavior, has advantages since it promotes durability and permanence of the behavioral change.

Conducting Personal Effectiveness in groups has many advantages over its use in one-to-one, individual sessions. Clients or students are exposed to a variety of models; there is much variation and subtlety in social and emotional communication; each person has a unique style that is learned and polished over a period of time. The process of learning to socialize and express feelings in a group setting provides each member with a range of possible models to emulate. Because imitative learning occurs more effectively when the models have characteristics in common with the learner, the presence of peers as well as therapists facilitates the acquisition of new behaviors. Also, when new clients enter a group, they can quickly develop positive expectations for treatment by witnessing the progress reported and exhibited by veteran group members. Likewise, clients making slower progress or having greater behavioral deficits can learn from observing the improvement in others.

Another advantage provided by the group is the powerful effect of social reinforcement in learning. Group members and therapists can strengthen appropriate behaviors and weaken maladaptive behaviors by giving the client positive and critical feedback. Practicing communication skills in a group also facilitates transfer or generalization of the practiced behavior to real-life situations. Transfer or generalization of newly learned behavior is improved by tailoring the learning situation to fit the natural situations that the person will encounter outside of the group. The group setting bears similarities to many situations in life where a person has opportunities to put into practice expressions of feeling and social contact; for example, at parties, meetings, classes, home, and work. Also, a person who learns a new skill is more likely to use it in situations that resemble the learning setting. Although the presence of a group may initially inhibit some clients or students, it is also true that moderately stressful conditions for learning closely approximate the stress found in real-life situations. If a client does well in a therapy group, there is a good chance that he will also do well in family, social, and work groups. Rather than provide a client a haven from the real world, Personal Effectiveness emphasizes real-life situations and their mastery through speech and action.

Training Steps

The process of Personal Effectiveness involves a systematic series of steps which are carefully followed for each group member in turn:

1. Problems that a person has in communicating and in expressing feelings are identified. This is done by helping the person specify the "where, when, how, what, and with whom" of the problem situation. For those who are comfortable with their social inadequacies, problem identification must be a joint enterprise with family, friends, or other informants. For example:

Matthew has marriage problems
    Where: at home
    When: usually as soon as he gets home from work
    How: because his wife nags him
    What: he can't express how he feels about it or adequately relate his complaints
With whom: his wife.

Jane has dating problems
    Where: at work
    When: whenever a man expresses interest in her
    How: whenever a man asks her to lunch
    What: she seems cold, verbally and nonverbally
With whom: the problem is worse with men she is attracted to.

Arthur annoys people

      Where: in stores
       When: whenever he feels he has been cheated
         How: because he bought some defective merchandise
        What: he begins to pound his fist and yell
With whom: the sales clerk.

2. The training goals are targeted. This is usually done by developing new behaviors:

>a. To rectify deficits in performance by strengthening desirable but weak behaviors. For example:

Matthew needs to learn assertive behaviors with his wife (voice loudness, eye contact, gestures).

Jane needs to learn behaviors that show interest and affection.

>b. To modulate excessive or overly intense emotional expressiveness. For example:

Jane may have to learn to control and reduce behavioral cues that are conveying disinterest or dislike.

Arthur needs to control aggressiveness by restraining his gestures, lowering his voice, and refraining from profanities.

3. The problem situation is simulated using the group members to role play or rehearse the relevant scenes. These should be scenes that have occurred in the recent past or are likely to occur in the near future. For example:

Matthew might rehearse a scene in which a client role playing the part of his wife nags him about not doing enough work around the house.

Pat could rehearse a recent job interview.

Arthur could try a scene in which a clerk refuses to take back a scratched record.

4. Learning techniques are used, such as explicit instructions, behavioral rehearsal, modeling, inserting and fading prompts,

Pat can't get a job

and shaping to gradually modify the client's expressive behavior. Components of the whole performance are added one-by-one, such as eye contact, facial expression, voice tone and loudness, posture, accessory body movements, and speech content. For example, after trying to stand up to his "wife":

Matthew watches the counselor model the scene for him. The counselor prompts *Pat* by using gestures to evoke facial expressions. The counselor models assertive behavior for *Arthur* and then provides verbal prompts (telling him what to say and do) while *Arthur* tries the scene again. Each small improvement is praised so that *Arthur's* behavior is gradually shaped to approximate the ultimate training goals.

5. The group gives feedback to the individual on his improved performance. Positive feedback for improvement rather than confrontation for failure is emphasized by the group leader. For example:

Matthew might be rated high on gestures but low on eye contact by the group. The high rating would be emphasized.

Arthur might receive high ratings, praise, and applause for a good performance.

16

6. The student is given an assignment to practice the behaviors, in real-life situations, that he has learned in the group setting. Group approval is used at subsequent sessions to reinforce successes. For example:

Matthew's assignment might be to refuse two unreasonable requests from his wife.

Tim could be asked to initiate three conversations.

Arthur might be asked to buy and then return some clothes.

Uses for Personal Effectiveness

Personal Effectiveness has been used successfully with over a thousand clients in the Day Treatment Center and the Outpatient Clinic of the Oxnard Community Mental Health Center, the psychiatric inpatient unit of Ventura General Hospital, the UCLA Neuropsychiatric Institute, and Camarillo State Hospital. The methods also have been effectively integrated into training programs for teachers; management development seminars for executives and supervisors; educational workshops for parents learning child-rearing skills; consciousness raising groups for women; training programs for indigenous nonprofessionals who will do community organization and family counseling; and seminars for trainees in psychiatry, psychology, social work, rehabilitation, and nursing.

Personal Effectiveness may also be used as part of curricula for emotional development in elementary and high schools. Too many youngsters go through their childhood and adolescence without ever learning effective ways to converse, to communicate, or to express their feelings. By employing the Personal Effectiveness approach in schools, our educational system could possibly prevent a significant degree of emotional and social impairment found among adults. With the severe shortage of qualified mental health and counseling professionals, prevention of emotional disorders is critically important.

Although Personal Effectiveness is highly relevant in schools, in training programs for workers in the human service fields, and for personnel development in business and government, its greatest current application has been with patients and clients in mental health facilities. Almost all people who come for treatment in psychiatric, psychological or counseling settings have major deficits in their social relationships and their ability to express their feelings. They have not acquired the communicative skills normally shown by others and they do not have the means to remedy their deficiencies. They frequently fail to take an active part in their families, in work, and in recreation; rather, they allow the world to pass them by. The goal of Personal Effectiveness is to teach these people to plan and to practice for success in their person-to-person contacts, and to generalize social and emotional training into real-life settings.

Examples of actual assignments that have been set for clients include the following:

Introducing oneself to a stranger

Inviting a neighbor over for coffee

Asking a foreman to repeat his job instructions for clarity

Calling a recreation department for information

Expressing enthusiasm and desire for help to a vocational rehabilitation counselor

Expressing affection to a husband

Asking a girl for a date

Requesting to drive the family car

Telling a roommate to bathe more often

Confronting a subordinate at work with poor performance

Selling oneself at a job interview

Requesting attention from a waitress

Confronting someone who persistently cheats at games

Returning food that has been poorly prepared in a cafe

Getting past the receptionist at the welfare office

Insisting that one's doctor explain his treatment fully and clearly

Giving verbal feedback on the kinds of lovemaking that one enjoys or dislikes

Saying "No!" to teenage friends who want to go joyriding

Telling one's mother that there will be no more taking sides in parental squabbles

Asking wife out to dinner

Greeting staff members spontaneously at the start of each day.

How effective are the procedures used in Personal Effectiveness in helping people reach their goals? While a review of the research on Assertion Training and other systematic behavioral approaches to communication and emotional expression is beyond the scope of this manual, interested readers can check the references in the Annotated Bibliography (p. 151) for an up-to-date catalog of outcome studies.

The authors conducted an evaluation of 100 consecutively rehearsed scenes that reflected goals set by clients at the Oxnard Day Treatment Center. The types of goals were similar to those listed above. The clients' self-reports were used as the criterion of "success" for the first 50 goals and 78 percent of these homework assignments were claimed to have been completed. During the next 50 assignments (to carry out a rehearsed behavior) research assistants accompanied the clients into their homes and communities to observe the results directly. Observations indicated that 80 percent of the rehearsed assignments were actually carried out. During the past three years of conducting Personal Effectiveness at the Oxnard Mental Health Center, 65-85 percent of over one thousand clients have reported success in completing their assignments. However, the exact percentage rate of success varies with the degree of difficulty of the behavioral goals and chosen assignments.

Content Guide

This manual has been prepared so that personnel in the helping professions can learn Personal Effectiveness and apply the procedures in their own places of work. The text is divided into three major sections corresponding to the three phases of one group session:

1. *The Planning Meeting;* prior homework assignments are discussed and reinforced contingent upon successful completion, and goals for the day's session are planned.

2. *The Training Session;* problematic, real-life situations are simulated, behavior is rehearsed by clients, and therapeutic interventions are made.

3. *The Evaluation Meeting;* clients' and staff's performances are discussed and evaluated with mutual supervision and feedback for improving skills in the training process.

Detailed and graphic descriptions of staff and client activities during each phase are provided. The careful reader should gain a grasp of the underlying principles and specific techniques of Personal Effectiveness. Readers with experience as therapists and counselors should be able to understand and apply the methods creatively within the context of their own programs and clinical styles. In addition, Personal Effectiveness can be readily added to existing repertoires of clinical and counseling skills. The methods are practical and pragmatic and do not require a commitment to a philosophy or theory of treatment and human behavior. The specific techniques outlined for group leaders, counselors, or therapists will be enhanced when they adapt them to their current ways of interacting with clients and students. It is hoped that presenting Personal Effectiveness to the professional public will add to the growing eclecticism in the helping professions.

To promote learning, this manual invites active involvement from the reader by providing practice exercises, questions, answers, and feedback. Questions follow each of the three major sections in the text. Some questions are general, more for the purpose of stimulating creative thought than for reviewing specific information; they are noted with an asterisk (*) and are not followed by any suggested answers.

While the manual provides all of the necessary information for learning Personal Effectiveness, the reader's experience will be amplified if he reads the manual with others under the direction of an instructor and views the demonstration film which provides a more graphic introduction.

Chapter 2
The Planning Meeting

Planning a Personal Effectiveness Session

The Planning Meeting takes place just prior to the actual Training Session and is held in a room large enough to seat all of the participating clients and staff. The reasons for this session are listed below:

1. To describe the purposes and operation of Personal Effectiveness to new clients.

2. To introduce new trainees to the group.

3. To obtain clients' reports on their real-life "homework" assignments from the previous session.

4. To provide feedback on clients' reports.

5. To plan the goals for the upcoming session's behavioral rehearsals.

Each of these five activities is described below with illustrative, client-counselor dialogues. It is very important not only *to understand* the procedures but also to be able *to carry them out.* Descriptions and illustrations cannot effectively accomplish this without the reader's active participation. We suggest that each of the activities in Personal Effectiveness be practiced with a number of role playing clients. One way of gaining this practice is to bring together a small group of colleagues for a simulated Personal Effectiveness session. Sample problems are described below. Readers are also encouraged to create their own scenes, cases, or clients and then to work through the procedures by actively role playing the make-believe scene.

Ann is a college sophomore having difficulty standing up for her opinions and ideas in class even when she is sure she is correct. In other situations she doesn't have this problem.

Russ has a hard time asking favors of people. This is his third Personal Effectiveness session. He failed to carry out an assignment to ask several people for matches. He wishes to practice asking a neighbor to drive him to a garage to pick up his car.

Jim is a new student who has a difficult time expressing affection toward his wife.

Felicia's husband always decides what they will watch on TV and Felicia would like to be able to watch some shows that she prefers.

LaVerne's former landlord has refused to return her cleaning deposit of $50.00 and claims that she has damaged things that were already damaged when she moved in. LaVerne would like to practice the scene with a female; her landlord is a male.

Robert is a relatively new client who seems to be very shy and withdrawn. He rarely initiates conversations with staff or other clients.

Dorothy would like to be able to accept and give criticism more easily. She is rather adamant about role playing with only one particular client in the Personal Effectiveness group.

Jacob is a new student who has had trouble "selling himself" in job interviews. He is eager to work on this interaction.

Danny has difficulty expressing his anger reasonably. He is making good progress and would like to work on a scene involving his reaction to a waiter's spilling coffee on him.

Sue socializes poorly, is unable to ask others to do things with her (e.g., going to the movies, shopping). This is her second Personal Effectiveness session but she is reluctant to do a scene.

Orienting Clients' Expectations

Since new clients probably will be joining the group at each session, you should begin the meeting with a brief orienting description of, and rationale for, Personal Effectiveness. This also refreshes current members about the purposes of training. Setting positive and clear expectations for the group facilitates subsequent learning. The description should be concise but thorough, and in simple, everyday language. Try to prompt veteran group members to assist in giving the description so that they get used to speaking out in a group and also so that new members get a peer's view of the training. An explanation of Personal Effectiveness should include mention of the following items:

1. What behaviors are practiced (facial expression, eye contact, use of hands, posture, voice tone, loudness and verbal content).

2. How behaviors are rehearsed (prompts, coaching, feedback, rehearsals, modeling).

3. Why behaviors are dealt with as primary targets rather than feelings or attitudes (because of the assumption that changes in behavior precede changes in feelings).

4. The requirement that all clients participate to some degree.

5. Ratings of rehearsals (positive feedback stressed).

6. Homework assignments (for practicing in the real world and choosing constructive, functional behavioral goals).

The following dialogue is an example of an orientation to Personal Effectiveness given by a counselor (C) and clients.

C: Welcome again to Tuesday morning Personal Effectiveness. I hope you're ready to get going. We've got a lot to cover in our session today. There are a few new faces so I think it would be a good idea to begin by talking about Personal Effectiveness for a few minutes and telling our new people what we're going to do during the session. Personal Effectiveness is a way of helping people to get along better with others and to express themselves better to others. We do this by concentrating on a number of things you do when you're talking to people. Bill, why don't you tell us what we work on during Personal Effectiveness.

Bill: Well, we try to use our hands more when we talk to people and also to look at them.

C: Very good, Bill. Karen, can you think of anything else?

Karen: No, I don't think so.

C: How about facial expressions, Karen?

Karen: Oh yes, we try to use our eyes and nod our heads and smile when we talk.

C: OK, fine. We work on a number of things that can help us to express our ideas and feelings. Mary, how do we practice these things?

Mary: Usually two of us go to the center of the room and pretend to be in the situation that we'd like to practice, like dating or talking to a boss or a neighbor. Sometimes one of the counselors shows us what to do and we try to imitate it. Sometimes we pretend we're the "other" person, like our boss.

C: Good; we rehearse scenes with the help of other clients and counselors and we concentrate on the types of behaviors we just talked about. We have one important rule here: everybody participates. If this is your first session, you may just watch this time to get a better understanding of our procedures, but everyone else will be involved. Don't be afraid to volunteer in a scene; you don't have to wait to be called on. One good thing about Personal Effectiveness is that we can help ourselves and we can also help each other. We do this by role playing for each other and also by rating each other after each rehearsal. Frank, would you like to talk about the ratings?

Frank: After a scene we rate things like posture, eye contact, and voice loudness from one to five by putting up our fingers.

C: That's right, Frank. I should point out, too, that we're not here to criticize but to help, so we try to point out good parts of a performance rather than being critical and picky. Also, we have you practice homework assignments out of class. You may want to work on things in here that you can try in real situations so that you can prepare yourself here for problems you have outside. You can try all sorts of things which may be difficult for you. We *do* try, though, to emphasize constructive situations like standing up for your rights as opposed to destructive things like getting back at someone who's taken advantage of you.

It should be noted that the counselor makes certain that all of the major points are covered, filling in the gaps when necessary, and also that he summarizes and restates the clients' descriptions.

Practice Exercise 1

Pretend you are in a Personal Effectiveness group with one person role playing a counselor and the others role playing clients. Give a brief but complete description of Personal Effectiveness and then discuss the strong points and shortcomings of your orientation exercise. Run through the description again with different people playing the counselor's role. Follow each scene with a discussion. Be sure to cover these points:

1. Which behaviors are practiced.

2. How behaviors are rehearsed.

3. Why behaviors are dealt with.

4. The participation requirement.

5. Ratings of scenes.

6. Homework assignments.

7. Inducing favorable, therapeutic expectations.

Introducing New Clients

New clients are introduced and a brief description of their problems and goals is given. This helps to ease new people into the group and provides information for other counselors to assist in treating them. An example of a counselor's (C) introduction is given below:

C: I'd like you all to meet Joan. This is Joan's first Personal Effectiveness session and I'd like to welcome her to our group. Joan, can you tell us a little about the problems that have brought you to the center?

Joan: My neighbors mostly.

C: How do they bother you?

Joan: They're nosey.

C: What kinds of things do they do?

Joan: Well, they're always asking me about my husband's work, our bills, the kids, you know, just all of my personal affairs.

C: How would you like to deal with them?

Joan: I'd like to be able to tell them to mind their own business, but I'm afraid of starting trouble.

C: I think we can probably help you to deal more effectively with your neighbors so that you can get them to mind their own business without offending them. This is something that we can start working on but for today, Joan, I'd just like you to watch what goes on and next time you can become more involved.

The client contributed to the fomulation of treatment goals with the assistance of the counselor. When the client defines his own problems, he achieves a greater sense of involvement in the training.

Practice Exercise 2

Work as a group and take turns role playing the counselor and various clients. Introduce new clients and assist them when deciding on their treatment goals. Be careful about imposing goals upon them by putting words in their mouths. Also, discuss each introduction before practicing another one. See Figure 1, page 28.

Obtaining Clients' Reports on Previous Assignments

Following the description of Personal Effectiveness and the introduction of new people, each counselor asks his clients to report on their previous week's assignments. The reporting procedure accomplishes the following goals:

1. Motivates clients to carry through on real-life assignments.

2. Allows for constructive group feedback.

3. Provides counselors with information on the clients' progress.

4. Facilitates the planning of the session's activities.

Clients are encouraged to provide explicit and detailed accounts of their assignments; to tell exactly:

1. What they did.

2. What others did.

3. How they felt.

4. What happened as a result of their assigned task.

Figure 1   Flow Chart Depicting the Orientation of Members in the Planning Meeting, the Opening Session of a Personal Effectiveness Meeting

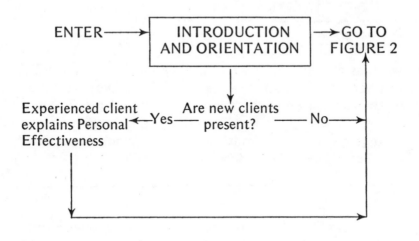

If necessary, counselors (C) should ask specific questions and prompt the client to be more explicit. Reports that are detailed are more likely to be accurate and reliable than reports which are phrased in generalities. Two samples of reports on assignments follow. The first includes most of the necessary details; the second client begins vaguely and must be prompted to be more specific.

C: Doug, you were supposed to ask your landlord about fixing a leaking faucet that you had brought to his attention last month. How did that go?

Doug: Well, I put it off for a few days because I was nervous about it, but I finally decided to talk to him on Friday.

C: And what happened?

Doug: I knocked on his door and he was watching TV. At first I felt like telling him that I'd come back some other time, but I decided not to. I told him that my faucet was still leaking and that he had had plenty of time to get to it. I asked him when he would fix it and he said sometime over the weekend. I asked him for a day and a time so I would be sure to be home, but he said he wasn't sure exactly when he could do it. I was starting to feel like giving up, but I looked straight at him and said, "Look, you've been telling me the same thing for weeks now and I'd like a specific time when you'll come over and fix the faucet." He started to say something about it being a bad weekend and I pointed at him and said, "If you can put off maintaining this place, I can put off paying the rent just as easily. I'd like to stay on good terms with you, but I have to insist on your doing your job." That seemed to do it because he agreed to be over Saturday morning. He showed up and fixed it, apologized for not doing it sooner, and asked if anything else needed repair.

The next client is vague and the counselor intervenes from time to time until she becomes more specific and detailed in her reporting of the events in her assignment.

C: Jane, would you like to tell us what happened when you asked your neighbor to keep her dog out of your yard? As I recall, her dog kept coming through the fence and digging in your garden.

Jane: Well, I asked her and at first she sort of ignored me, but then I convinced her to chain him up.

C: How did you go about asking her?

Jane: I just asked her.

C: Did you call her up, or see her in person?

Jane: I went over to her house.

C: And then what?

Jane: I told her about the dog.

C: What did you say?

Jane: I said that I was getting a little upset at her dog because he was ruining my garden.

C: Then what did she say?

Jane: Well, she sort of put me off.

C: What exactly did she say?

Jane: She told me that her dog is always getting out of the yard, but that he doesn't really do any harm.

C: Go on.

Jane: I told her that he may be harmless as far as she's concerned, but my flowers probably don't agree.

C: What did she say then?

Jane: She said she couldn't believe that her dog would dig up flowers.

C: How did you react to that?

Jane: I felt nervous, but I didn't give up.

C: Good, what did you do?

Jane: I told her that she could come over and take a look at the flowers if she wanted to; but she said she took my word for it. Then I asked her what she would do about it, and she said that she'd try to keep her dog in the yard. I asked her how she planned to do that and she said she'd keep an eye on him. I asked her if she ever thought of chaining him and she said no but that it might be a good idea.

C: Did she do anything about it?

Jane: I saw her Saturday and asked her if she thought anymore about chaining the dog. She said her husband had bought a chain and he was going to hook it up.

Providing Feedback

When a client reports the successful completion of an assignment, the counselor and group provide immediate, ample, and enthusiastic social reinforcement. Praise, encouragement, or even applause should be given for any improvement, no matter how slight. In addition, if a token economy is in operation, the tokens or points can be dispensed and later exchanged for tangible rewards. Giving positive feedback encourages further real-life attempts at social expressiveness and raises the morale and commitment of all the group members as well.

Successes are rewarded with approval from the counselors and the other members. Reports of failure or lack of effort are not dwelt on; effort is always acknowledged and rewarded. In cases of failure, the client should be encouraged to try again or possibly to try a less difficult assignment. Feedback should be positive. Criticism and confrontation

Therapist and group provide enthusiastic feedback to client who has just reported successful completion of a homework assignment

over failures are avoided. The counselor should always try to find something positive in the client's account to reward and acknowledge.

Below are examples of the kinds of comments that can be made *following successful completion* of an assignment:

"Good!"
"Wonderful!"
"Excellent!"
"Terrific!"
"You're really doing great."
"You're really coming along."
"I'm so pleased at the progress you're making."
"I think that deserves some applause."

In cases of *failure despite effort* the counselor can say something like the following:

"I think with a little more practice you'll be able to do that."
"We can't always expect to be successful right away, but it's good that you tried."
"I'm really happy that you tried."

Negatively toned comments, such as the following, *should be avoided:*

"I think you can do better than that."
"That was OK, but not quite good enough."
"There was only one thing that you did that could have been improved." (It is better for the counselor to forget about it.)
"That wasn't a very good approach except for one thing." (It is better for the counselor to simply praise that one thing.)
"That wasn't very good."

The counselor should take advantage of the group's reinforcing potential by encouraging clients to comment upon each other's reports. To ensure positive feedback, the counselor

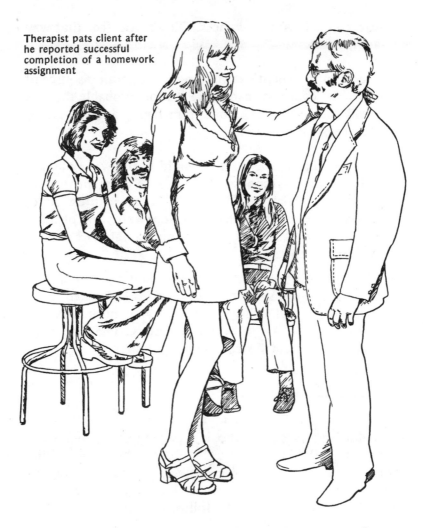

can ask for comments solely on the positive aspects of someone's report. For example, if a client were successful in standing up for his rights in one of three assignments, the counselor would ask for the group's reaction to the successful assignment. Even if the client did not meet with success, the counselor (C) would still focus on something positive, such as effort. See Figure 2, page 35. The following is a good example:

C: I think you were on the right track for a while, Jim, especially when you said that you made sure to keep eye contact with your boss. Didn't you feel that way too, Alex?

The people in the client's environment are another source of feedback. The counselor can make it more probable that the client will get positive reactions from family and friends by following these guidelines:

1. Setting up assignments that would likely evoke pleasurable, approving responses. Examples of assignments with a high potential for "pay-off" are the expression of affection or other positive emotions, initiating pleasant social activities such as lunch or dinner dates, or athletic or leisure activities.

2. Meeting with the family and explaining the importance of social reinforcement. The family can be asked to become aware of the client's attempts at emotional expressiveness and to be generous with praise and encouragement for even small steps in the right direction.

Practice Exercise 3

Pair off with a colleague and take turns role playing the "counselor" and a client who is reporting on a homework assignment. Discuss your efforts before switching roles. If the report was not specific and complete, try the scene again, asking for the necessary additional information. Make sure you find out in detail about the following points:

1. What the client did and said and how it was done.

2. What others did and said.

3. How the client felt.

4. What happened as a result of the assignment.

The person role playing "counselor" gives the "client" feedback after his report. Be sure to stress accomplishments and to be positive.

Figure 2   Flow Chart Depicting the Processing of Reported Assignments by the Leader in the Planning Phase of a Personal Effectiveness Group Session

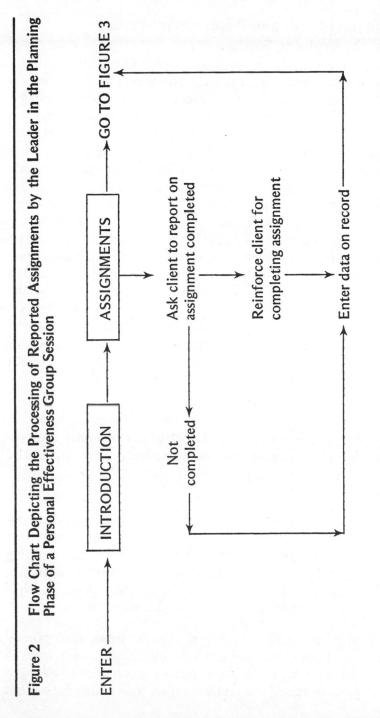

ENTER ⟶ INTRODUCTION ⟶ ASSIGNMENTS ⟶ GO TO FIGURE 3

Ask client to report on assignment completed

Not completed

Reinforce client for completing assignment

Enter data on record

Choosing Goals and Planning Activities
for the Training Session

During the Planning Meeting each client formulates, with the help of the counselor, the goals and scenes he will work on during the Training Session. Clients are encouraged to participate actively in choosing their behavioral goals for the session. When helping the client decide upon training goals, the counselor should make use of all information which he has on that person, including behavioral assessments, interview data, family reports, biographical data, and reports from previous treatment experiences. The counselor should come into a Personal Effectiveness session with full knowledge of his clients' assets and deficits and then guide their choice of scenes in light of this knowledge. Practice scenes usually overlap with real-life assignments; that is, the scenes practiced in the session correspond to those to be carried out during the upcoming week. See Figure 3.

Some scenes and assignments are better than others. Several criteria can be used to determine which of several possible scenes should be chosen. Training should deal with the following elements:

1. Positive and constructive behaviors; for example, asking for a raise as opposed to talking back to a boss; requesting a desired change in the actions of a spouse instead of arguing or complaining about past unpleasantness.

2. Functional behaviors; that is, they should provide maximum payoff for the client in the real world. For example, asking a friend to lunch as opposed to asking for a favor; expressing affection as opposed to criticism; requesting a job interview rather than talking with a staff member.

3. High frequency behaviors; that is, those that can be practiced often. For example, initiating conversations as opposed to returning defective merchandise; asking a boss to repeat instructions rather than asking for a raise.

Figure 3 Flow Chart Depicting the Procedure for Developing Scenes for the Behavioral Rehearsals that Clients Will Engage in During the Training Session

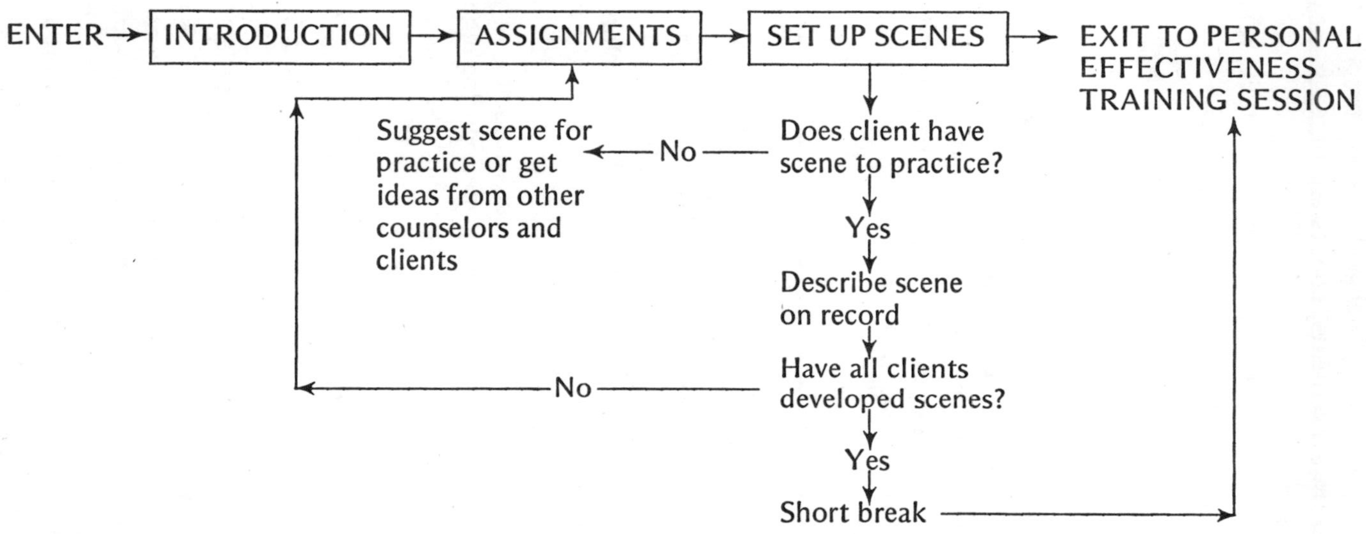

ENTER → INTRODUCTION → ASSIGNMENTS → SET UP SCENES → EXIT TO PERSONAL EFFECTIVENESS TRAINING SESSION

Does client have scene to practice?

No → Suggest scene for practice or get ideas from other counselors and clients

Yes

Describe scene on record

Have all clients developed scenes?

No

Yes

Short break

37

In addition to choosing behaviors to be practiced and then carried out in assignments, clients are urged to bring up any other difficulties they have been having with people and to work on any interpersonal activity that they would like to improve.

Practice Exercise 4

Pair off with a partner and take turns role playing the "counselor" and the "clients" described on page 22. Decide upon goals and scenes to be rehearsed during the Training Session and discuss the adequacy of the planned scenes. Be sure you are dealing with *positive, functional,* and *high frequency behaviors.*

Finally, as the Planning Meeting ends, directors and recorders of scenes for the day's Personal Effectiveness session are chosen from among the available staff. Counselors rotate the tasks of actually directing and leading Personal Effectiveness sessions and recording performances on each client's Record Sheet (see Appendix, p. 141). Other counselors or staff members can alternate directing scenes during the Training Session. Capable volunteers can be usefully enlisted as recorders, directors, and role models. The Planning Meeting usually ends by choosing someone to record the five-point performance ratings on a blackboard. A Planning Meeting for ten clients in a group generally lasts for 20 to 30 minutes. A five- to ten-minute break then precedes the training.

It is advisable to appoint a team leader for overall responsibility and managerial authority for the sessions. The leader should have a good knowledge of Personal Effectiveness and have supervisory and program evaluation skills. If such a person is not immediately available, someone with the qualifications of a leader should be retained on a consultant basis.

Review Questions

Answer the following questions in the spaces provided and compare your response with the suggested answers on pages 44-45. Discuss your answers with colleagues and reread parts of the manual if you feel it is necessary. Questions with an asterisk are open-ended and no suggested answers are given.

1. What are the five major activities and functions of the Planning Meeting?

2. What are some of the reasons for describing Personal Effectiveness at the beginning of the Planning Meeting?

3. What seven features of Personal Effectiveness should be included in the orientation and description of the procedures?

4. What is the best way to formulate treatment goals for new clients?

5. What are the reasons for having clients report on their real-life assignments?

6. Which four pieces of information should be included in a client's detailed report of his assignment?

7. How should a counselor handle a client who is describing an assignment in loose, vague terms?

8. When giving feedback, how does the counselor respond to successful reports of completed assignments? To failures?

9. How can a counselor increase the likelihood of positive reactions to a behavioral assignment from a client's family or friends?

10. What should be the counselor's attitude and actions toward a client's involvement when planning training activities?

11. Which three characteristics should targeted behavioral goals possess?

*12. How would you feel about Personal Effectiveness if you were a new client who had just heard a description of it? How would you feel about seeing and hearing other clients give the description?

*13. Do you think that it is a good idea to let clients partici-
pate in formulating treatment goals?

*14. Do you think positive feedback is better than negative
feedback? Why?

*15. Do you think that the Planning Meeting fails to cover
any important points? If you were a new client, how
would you feel at the end of the Planning Meeting?

Suggested Answers

1. Five major activities are given below:

   1. To describe the purposes and operation of Personal Effectiveness to new clients.
   2. To introduce new clients to the group.
   3. To obtain clients' reports on their real-life homework assignments.
   4. To provide feedback on the clients' reports.
   5. To plan the activities for the upcoming session.

2. Following are three reasons for describing Personal Effectiveness at the beginning of the Planning Meeting:

   1. For the sake of new members.
   2. To refresh old members about the purpose of training.
   3. To set positive and clear expectations of what is to come.

3. The seven features of Personal Effectiveness that should be included in the orientation and description of the procedures are given below:

   1. Which behaviors are practiced.
   2. How behaviors are rehearsed.
   3. Why observable behaviors are dealt with.
   4. The participation requirement.
   5. Ratings of rehearsals.
   6. Homework assignments.
   7. Inducing favorable, therapeutic expectations.

4. The best way to develop treatment goals is to allow the client to formulate his own goals with the assistance of a counselor.

5. Some of the reasons for having the client report on real-life assignments are given below:

   1. It motivates clients to carry through on assignments.
   2. It allows for constructive group feedback.
   3. It provides counselors with information on the client's progress.
   4. It facilitates planning of the session's activities.

6. The client's report should include the following details.

   1. What he did.
   2. What others did.

3. How he felt.
4. What happened as a result of his assigned task.

.7. If a client is giving a vague report, the counselor should intervene and ask specific questions and prompt him to be more specific.

8. When giving feedback, successes are emphasized and greeted with approval while reports of failure or lack of effort are minimized. In cases of failure, encourage the client to try again or formulate a less difficult assignment. The counselor should be generous with praise for success.

9. Positive reactions from a client's family or friends may be ensured by the following procedure:

   1. Setting up assignments that would be likely to evoke pleasurable responses.
   2. Meeting with the family and explaining the importance of social reinforcement.

10. Clients should be encouraged to participate in planning goals and in the Training Session.

11. Targeted behavioral goals should be *positive, functional,* and *high frequency behaviors.*

Practice Exercises

Dick is a client who is having a difficult time with his friends because he feels that they are always taking advantage of him. Take turns role playing Dick and his counselor (C). Read aloud the introductory dialogues below and improvise where indicated to complete the action satisfactorily as in a Planning Meeting. Discuss each exercise before going on to the next one.

Exercise 5

C: I'd like everyone to meet Dick. Dick, you mentioned to me that you're having problems with your friends. What do you mean by that?

Dick: They get on my nerves.

C: In what way?

Dick: I don't know, they just don't seem like very good friends I guess.

Improvise. . . .

Exercise 6

C: Dick, you were supposed to tell your friend Bob to go home when you were ready to make yourself dinner. You mentioned that he always sticks around and you end up feeding him. How did you do?

Dick: Pretty good.

C: Good; what happened?

Dick: Well, I told him to take off when suppertime came.

Improvise. . . .

Exercise 7

C: Is there anything in particular you'd like to work on today, Dick?

Dick: I'd like to figure out a way to get some free meals out of Bob the way he always mooches off me.

Improvise. . . .

Chapter 3
The Training Session

Following the break, the clients are divided into groups of four to fifteen members. Each group has at least two co-leaders or counselors to share directing and recording duties. Groups of more than fifteen are unwieldy and should be avoided. The room should be large enough for comfortable seating in a circle of chairs with enough space in the middle for acting out the interpersonal scenes and situations. A blackboard is located at one end of the room.

Ideally, each counselor works with those clients for whom he is primarily responsible; that is, each counselor's caseload should be assigned to the small group which he co-leads. This maximizes continuity and individualization of training. However, if sufficiently briefed in advance, a substitute trainer can satisfactorily direct scenes for the clients of an absent counselor.

The primary activity of the Training Session is the rehearsal of verbal and nonverbal aspects of expressive behaviors. The co-leaders' goals are to encourage each client to practice ways of improving his performance and skills in social situations. This is generally achieved by a three-part sequence. First, during a dry run behavioral rehearsal the participant recapitulates the problem situation in role playing. The leader uses this initial run-through as an opportunity to identify the deficits and excesses in the participant's social and emotional performance. Second, modeling is introduced to demonstrate an improved method of social expression. Third, during a rerun or replay the participant attempts to gradually integrate the modeled behavior into his repertoire with the help of prompts and positive feedback.

Major emphasis is on the *nonverbal components* of emotional behavior in person-to-person communication. For instance, training someone to express affection and tenderness focuses more upon facial expression, voice tone, eye contact, and body movement than on the actual choice of words and phrases. When teaching a client to better express a reasonable grievance, posture, hand gestures, and volume of voice are emphasized more than the semantics of the verbal message. For each client, the counselor or co-leader sets up a scene, gets the client to rehearse, intervenes with modeling and prompting, and provides feedback. This section of the manual will deal with each of the following items:

1. Setting the stage for scenes.

2. Stock scenes.

3. Techniques for teaching.

4. Tricks for treatment.

5. Strategies for intervention.

6. Giving real-life assignments.

Setting the Stage

When the Planning Meeting ends, each participant has a good idea of what he will practice. Each participant takes a turn setting up a scene and taking a dry run in role playing. The leader either asks for a volunteer or chooses someone to take a turn setting the stage for a scene. New members, in the group for the first time, are often allowed to watch without having to develop their own scene. Observing others and participating as surrogates in role playing very effectively diminishes performance anxiety and promotes vicarious learning of expectations and social skills. When it's time to practice, the leader asks the client to describe the problem situation again, this time in greater detail. Details help make the scene realistic and give everyone in the group a clear understanding of exactly what is to take place. Graphic descriptions of the people involved in the problem situation, their actions and anticipated reactions, and the setting make the session more interesting for everyone. Other members in the group will recognize themselves and their own problems as each participant describes his situation.

Because some people try to talk a scene to death instead of practicing, the counselor or leader must provide flexible guidance in eliciting the

Who?
What?
When?
Where?
How?

of the scene or situation. Forget the "Why" and guide the participant toward specific portrayal of some recent example of the problem situation, or of an example that is anticipated in the near future. Choose situations for rehearsal that occur often in the person's life. Avoid listening to or probing for reasons "why" the participant has difficulty with the emotions, communication, and people depicted in the scene. Speculation on the motives only leads to boredom and endless talk, deterring the client and the leader from moving on to remedial action. Remember, the task is to get to the point quickly. Get the scene on, get it off, and do it again. Specifics, action, and repetition are the soul of learning. Don't get bogged down in redundant details, but get the client to provide enough background information to make the scene real. For example, find out if the situation requires the role players to stand up or sit down, or if the scene requires a surrogate who is old or young, or if some props might be helpful, such as in the case of playing a scene where the participant is returning defective merchandise to a store.

Encouraging the participant to set the stage with graphic details makes him feel that he is helping to plan and manage the treatment process. The mystique of psychotherapy is abandoned by involving the client as an active agent in his own therapy. The counselor assists the client to select and develop good scenes to practice without wasting valuable time on trivial or harmful behavioral goals.

Once the scene is properly described, the client picks another member of the group to serve as a surrogate for the role of the person in real life with whom he wants to improve communication or emotional expression. If the role played situation involves several people, the participant and the leader call upon several members of the group to enact the scene. When choosing surrogate role players, the client and the leader are guided by the *similarity rule:* the surrogates should have similar characteristics to the real-life individuals they are portraying. Characteristics of importance in establishing realism include age, sex, nonverbal behaviors, assertiveness, and communication style. Surrogates can be chosen as models of the actual people from among the staff or clients.

The surrogate needs to know the characteristics of the person whose role is being taken so that appearance and response style can be satisfactorily mimicked. If the surrogate is the client's husband, who is middle-aged and overbearing, then a middle-aged man should be chosen and told how to act by the client and the leader. While surrogates for role playing can be solicited through volunteers, the leader will many times find active selection more expedient and less anxiety provoking. The leader also will be in a better position to move the group into action with prompts, modeling, and feedback if he is standing up and moving around the room. Leadership in Personal Effectiveness requires an "out-of-the-seat," active therapist or counselor (see Figure 4).

Using other members of the group as surrogates for "interpersonal targets" produces a hidden bonus for social learning. The people taking others' roles practice a range of characters and behaviors. This loosens inhibitions and provides opportunities to gain experiences with new and different response styles. When a particular, significant other person is not involved in the problem situation, a useful strategy is to replay the same situation several times using different surrogates as role players. This approach fosters flexibility. The client, learning social skills by reacting to different kinds of "interpersonal targets," has a chance to try a variety of responses and styles, thereby building a broader behavioral repertoire. Practicing with a number of dissimilar role players facilitates generalization of the newly learned social skills to

Figure 4   Flow Chart for Setting the Stage to Practice a Scene in Personal Effectiveness

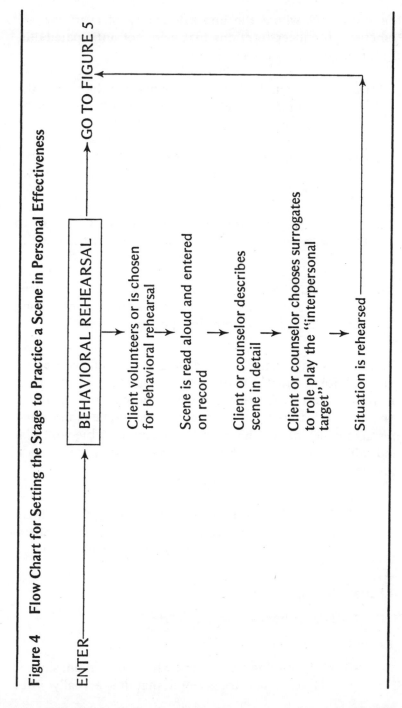

ENTER →

BEHAVIORAL REHEARSAL → GO TO FIGURE 5

Client volunteers or is chosen for behavioral rehearsal →

Scene is read aloud and entered on record →

Client or counselor describes scene in detail →

Client or counselor chooses surrogates to role play the "interpersonal target" →

Situation is rehearsed

53

the real world where the unpredictability of everyday life sometimes produces reactions that were not anticipated during the behavioral rehearsal. To summarize:

1. Describe in detail what is to take place in the scene—the "Who," "What," "When," "Where," and "How" of the problem situation.

2. Provide flexible guidance when supporting the client's active participation in choosing a scene and setting the stage for the scene.

3. Use role players who have characteristics similar to those with whom the client will interact in the real-life situation.

4. Use a number of role players reflecting different response styles when teaching skills that are not being applied to a specific, significant other person.

Following is an example of a scene being set up by a counselor (C) for a client, Charles, who complained of problems on his job. Part of Charles' problem resulted from his reluctance to ask his boss questions; consequently, he made many mistakes which caused his boss to become irritable with him and which, in turn, made Charles even more afraid to ask questions.

C: OK, Charles, we are going to work on the problem you have asking your boss to repeat the instructions he gives you. Who would you like to work with?

Charles: Maria.

C: Is your boss a woman, Charles?

Charles: No, a man.

C: Well why don't you work with a man, then, since it will be easier to pretend that it's actually your boss. How about you, Tom? Would you like to role play Charles' boss?

Tom: Sure.

C: Charles, tell us how your boss acts when he gives instructions? How does he talk and what does he do?

Charles: Well, he talks real loud so its hard to interrupt him, and he talks fast, too. Sometimes he paces back and forth.

C: Charles, you told us that your boss gave you some instructions last week regarding the time schedule of some shipments. You really didn't get it straight but you didn't ask him to repeat it. Would you like to try that scene now with Tom?

Charles: Can I also practice complaining to him about talking so fast when he gives directions?

C: Maybe we can work on that later, but for now let's just work on asking him to repeat himself. Whether he talks too fast or too slow, you still have to learn how to get the instructions straight. Tom, do you understand the situation? Give Charles a time schedule for some shipments; for instance: "Send out the Rochester shipment at 2:30, the Cleveland shipment at 3:50, and so on." When you play the scene, talk loud and fast and pace back and forth a little, too. OK?

Tom: OK.

C: Charles, I want you to stop Tom as soon as you lose track of the instructions. Then ask him to repeat what he's said. Remember to use hand gestures like putting up your hand to mean "stop" and also the gestures we've worked on to let Tom know that you'd like him to speak very slowly.

Notice that the counselor goes over each of the following points.

1. He promotes a detailed description of the scene for all participants.

2. He guides the choice of the scene when the client suggests a more difficult one.

3. He suggests that a male surrogate role play the boss since Charles' boss was a male.

4. He elicits the response style of the role played figure to make the performance more realistic.

Below is one more example with a client, Norma, who complained of a lack of privacy in her life. Her counselor questioned her about this and found out that part of Norma's problem was caused by one of her neighbors, who frequently used her telephone.

C: Let's try that scene with your neighbor today, Norma. OK? You said that you'd like to learn how to go about suggesting that she get her own phone. Who would you like to work with?

Norma: Annette.

C: Fine. Annette, would you like to role play Norma's neighbor?

Annette: Sure; what should I do?

C: Norma has mentioned before that her neighbor knocks on her door and asks to use her phone. Basically, that's what you'll do. Norma, can you tell us a little more about how your neighbor acts, and what she says when she comes to use your phone?

Norma: She usually walks right in before I even ask her in; then she starts dialing the phone while she's asking me if she can use it.

C: What does she usually say?

Norma: She usually has some "urgent" reason to use the phone, but the calls don't sound that important to me.

C: How does she act when she comes in?

Norma: She starts talking very fast about the call as soon as I open the door, then she just about runs to the phone and dials before I can say anything. By the time I can open my mouth she's already talking on the phone.

C: Annette, do you understand what to do?

Annette: Yes, I knock on the door and use the phone.

C: Right. But also act like you're in a hurry. Talk fast and walk quickly to the phone, talking all the time. Tell Norma that the call is about something very important.

Annette: OK, I can do that.

C: Good. Norma, when Annette starts walking in, use hand gestures to indicate that you want her to "wait a minute." Don't be afraid to interrupt her and ask her exactly why she has to use the phone. Stop her from dialing if you have to. Remember, you want to talk to her about the phone calls and you have to interrupt her before she makes the call.

Norma: What should I say then?

C: We can work on that later. For now just practice stopping her and asking her what the present call is for. After you learn to stop her, then you can practice suggesting that she get her own phone.

Practice Exercise 1

Pair off with another reader and alternate taking the role of client and counselor for the cases described on page 3. In each instance set up a scene and evaluate its adequacy on the basis of the four procedural points listed in the summary on page 54.

Stock Scenes

For Personal Effectiveness sessions with actual clients and "for practice" when training staff, a series of stock scenes may be used. These scenes may be used for the following reasons:

1. To "warm up" a group at any point in the Training Session.

2. To provide an objective assessment of clients' skills in expressive behaviors prior to goal setting.

3. To "break up" a session that has extended beyond the limits of the group members' learning capacities. Learning is impaired by practice periods that are too long, overly complex or repetitious.

Stock scenes should involve as many of the group at one time as is practical within the limits imposed by space. The choice of scenes is limited only by the imagination and creativity of the counselor and his group members. The scenes should be from everyday life and familiar to as many people as possible. Some suggestions are given below:

1. A movie line or other queue is arranged. One person in line sees newly arriving friends and invites them into the line ahead of others already there.

2. A secretary attempts to put off a client who desires an appointment.

3. A waitress serves food that should be unacceptable (burned steak, warm beer, a dirty dish).

4. A person arrives at a restaurant or hotel to find that his reservation has not been recorded and no table or room is ready for him.

5. A person returns a gift to a store with no sales slip and demands a *cash* refund, not a credit slip.

6. Someone returns for the fifth time to an auto service station to have the *same* problem repaired.

7. A person enters a new car salesroom, indicates no present plan to purchase a car, but requests a test drive.

8. A driver asks the gas station attendant to check the tire pressure, battery, oil, and to clean the windshield.

Techniques for Teaching Personal Effectiveness

Behavioral Rehearsal

Behavioral rehearsal is the core and framework for learning Personal Effectiveness. Brief scenes that depict problem situations are enacted in a manner that simulates the actual situation. People learn new skills through practice, and behavioral rehearsal provides substantial opportunities for practice. The other training techniques are used to *facilitate* the learning of social skills through behavioral rehearsal. Prompts, models, and rewards are used to evoke and strengthen an adaptive, constructive, and effective behavioral performance.

Behavioral rehearsal differs from other types of therapeutic techniques, such as psychodrama or group encounter, because the emphasis is placed on the client's goal-oriented, overt, verbal and nonverbal behavior rather than his feelings, catharsis, beliefs, or attitudes. Behavioral rehearsal is followed by positive feedback from the leader and group rather than by criticism and confrontation. As stated previously, the authors believe that desirable changes in feelings and attitudes follow behavioral changes.

Behavioral rehearsal is the vehicle for teaching language and conversational skills, emotional expressiveness and social, vocational, and recreational interactions. Table 2 (page 60), lists examples of the types of goals practiced for Personal Effectiveness. During behavioral rehearsal, participants execute scenes that were planned for the Personal Effectiveness session. The first time a person practices a scene, the "dry run," the counselor should observe carefully for both strengths and weaknesses in the performance. The counselor or leader makes the all-important assessment of the participant's initial level of social competence, paying particular attention to the nonverbal aspects of behavior. Nonverbal

Table 2   Goals of Personal Effectiveness Practiced in Behavioral Rehearsals

Language

1. Instructions: listening to and repeating instructions.
2. Conversation: initiating, continuing, concluding talk with a friend, relative or acquaintance where the object of social contact is to talk rather than to meet someone.
3. Information: giving or asking for information; conversation on a specific topic for purposes of information exchange.

Expression of Emotion

1. Facial and motor expressions: to show affection, anger, pleasure or irritation when appropriate in a social situation.
2. Affection: showing affection to another person.
3. Anger: expressing anger, irritation or annoyance.
4. Criticism: accepting and giving criticism.
5. Praise: accepting and giving praise.
6. Assertiveness: dealing with and overcoming the noncompliance of others; not complying with the unreasonable wishes of others.
7. Sadness: showing feelings of sorrow, regret and grief.

Social Interaction

1. Recreation: arranging to "get out" with a friend, relative or acquaintance for shopping, going to the movies; or, inviting others to one's home.
2. Social approach: meeting new people, arranging for dating or other social contact with the purpose of making new friends.
3. Personal request: asking a favor of a friend, relative or acquaintance.
4. Personal business: paying bills, making purchases, returning defective merchandise, dealing with social agencies and bureaucrats.

Employment

1. Interviews and follow-up: interviews for work; follow-up contacts for job-seeking; conversation about job; seeking volunteer work and educational opportunities in schools. Includes introductions for jobs.
2. Job skills: dealing with job supervisors, co-workers and subordinates; giving and accepting criticism and positive feedback; soliciting more complete instructions and feedback on performance.

behaviors, such as eye contact and vocal tone, communicate meaning and have impact on others even more than the literal content of the spoken words.

When the counselor is out of his seat, he's in a good position for viewing and hearing the participant's behavioral rehearsal. He can also plunge into the training process by

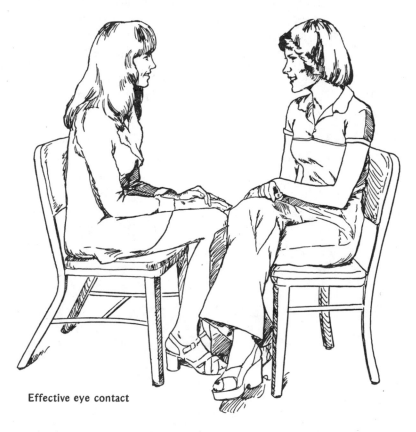

Effective eye contact

identifying the assets and deficiencies of the client's delivery. Skilled counselors and trainers, mindful of the inventory of nonverbal and verbal dimensions which are crucial for Personal Effectiveness, should ask themselves the following clinical questions as they monitor the dry run of their client or student:

1. Eye Contact. Does the client look at the person he is talking to?

2. **Use of Hands.** Does the client make use of hand gestures to emphasize points while talking?

3. **Facial Expression.** Does the client maintain facial expressions appropriate to the situation and the verbal message?

4. **Posture.** Does the client's posture communicate interest (or in some cases disinterest) in the other person? Does he incline his body slightly toward the person to show concern and interest? Does he face the person? How close to the person does he stand?

5. **Voice Loudness.** Is his voice audible or is it too soft or too loud?

6. **Voice Tone.** Does the client vary pitch or speak in a monotone? Does the voice sound nasal or whining?

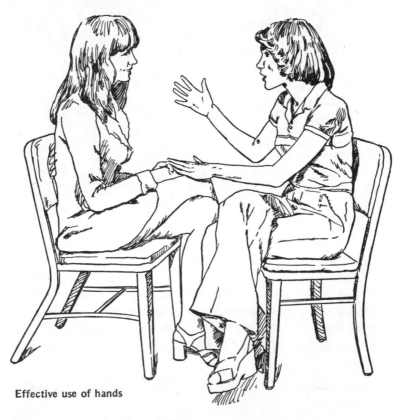

Effective use of hands

7. **Speech Fluency.** Is the client fluent? Is his speech free of mannerisms that show anxiety, or repetitions and "ahs" that reveal lack of certainty? Included here are periods of blocking, trailing off, pauses and other non-verbal elements of speech that interfere with communication.

The *way one sounds* is as important as the way one looks and what one says. People will sooner forget what you are wearing than what you sound like. Our ears are sound-sensitive and everyone has the vocal ability to cause a flight or fright reaction or to induce others to hear you out and pay close attention to your message. Nasality, stridency, and shrillness are to the ear what halitosis is to the nose. The voice does a great job getting good responses from people, but it also can make them turn away. The voice reflects an emotional state and is a barometer of feelings and self-confidence. Very competitive and angry people sound harsh and loud. Shy, insecure people speak in low tones and low intensity. Proper pitch is determined by good breath support and relaxation. As soon as a person becomes tense, the pitch rises. To get an idea of what you sound like to other people, put your nose in the middle of a magazine or into a corner of the room and talk into it. This exercise produces an amplification of your voice and will give you a better experience at hearing your own vocal tones.

In behavioral rehearsal, the counselor cuts the enactment of the dry-run scene as soon as enough observations are collected for identification of the client's strong and weak points on the nonverbal dimensions listed above. Scenes generally do not have to run more than a few minutes and it is preferable to keep them brief and focused. Instant feedback is given to the participant as soon as the scene ends. A good rule for giving feedback is to always start with positive comments. *Every time* a person rehearses, he should be given positive social feedback for the appropriate aspects of his performance. The counselor may have to stretch reality to find something to reward, but *the rule of positive feedback must not be ignored.* It should be done every time a client practices in Personal Effectiveness.

Immediately after the scene, ask three or four group members to give positive feedback for things that the participant did well. Be sure that the feedback is directed so that it is positive. The counselor can ensure this by structuring the group member's evaluation. "Jim, would you give Marcia some feedback on her *excellent* use of hands in that scene"; or "Tony's eye contact was *really good* that time. Did any of you see how *effectively* he used his hands, too?" The counselor trains all group members to attend to and remark on the positive aspects of each others' performances. This is best done by the counselor modeling, by giving positive feedback himself, and by cutting off criticism quickly but pleasantly.

Once positive feedback is given, the counselor and the group members can make constructive comments about how the participant might improve his manner of expression. These constructively critical suggestions should be phrased in a positive way that encourages the participant to try again. The counselor has an important job when modeling and structuring constructive criticism. He might say, "Pat, your

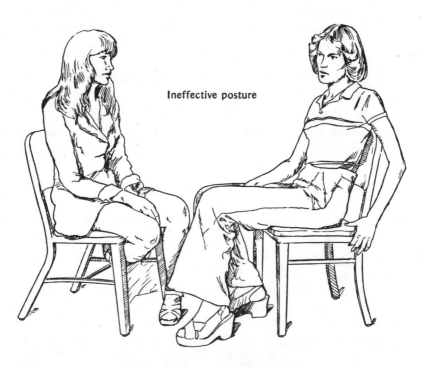

Ineffective posture

eye contact was good, but I'd like you to work on improving your posture." He should also focus on what the participant can do better next time rather than on what was done poorly. He picks out one, two, or at the most three features that can be improved. But he should not expect a lengthy and complicated critique to instigate change. Eye contact is almost always the *sine qua non* for Personal Effectiveness. The counselor builds up eye contact first before adding other features and chooses one or two salient aspects to work on before moving ahead to the next phase of training, the modeling procedure.

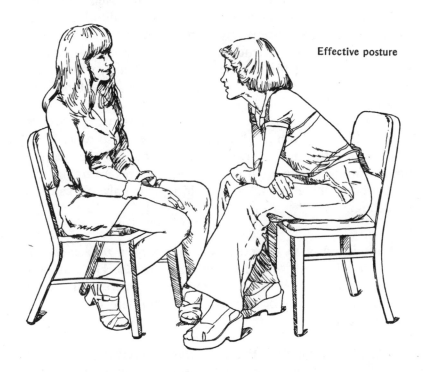

Effective posture

Modeling

Unless the client flawlessly rehearses a scene during the dry run, the counselor must step in and demonstrate how to manage the situation in a more effective manner. The dry run is almost always desirable since it permits the counselor to directly assess the client's initial level of interpersonal competence. However, at times with very resistant, shy and withdrawn individuals, it is like pulling teeth to get them out of their seats to run through an initial rehearsal of a scene. On such occasions the counselor can go directly into a demonstration of the client's problem situation by having someone else model the behavior. Watching a model, particularly a peer or fellow group member, makes it easier for the resistant client to become involved as an active participant.

After determining the member's social and emotional deficiencies in the dry run, the counselor can take the next step in the training procedure—modeling improved behavior. If Personal Effectiveness is being conducted within individual therapy, then the therapist must serve as the model. In group therapy, on the other hand, a variety of role models can be selected, including the counselors, other clients, volunteers, or even family members who are invited to attend the session.

Modeling makes use of the principle that a picture is worth a thousand words. Showing a client what to do is often a more effective and efficient teaching method than telling him. Although there are no strict guidelines regarding the use of a model, there are three situations which always call for modeling:

1. Modeling is an effective way of giving a *new member* some idea of what he's supposed to do. He may not understand how to behaviorally enact instructions to be more expressive or assertive, to show interest, or to look more relaxed.

2. When teaching relatively *complex behaviors*, modeling allows the client to see the entire behavioral pattern. For simple behaviors, verbal instructions may be sufficient.

3. Whether dealing with simple or complex behaviors, modeling allows the client to learn important *nonverbal, expressive qualities*. There is no easier or more effective

way to teach good use of gestures, eye contact, posture, and tone of voice than by modeling.

Modeling has been demonstrated to be an effective and relatively rapid means for bringing about changes in behavior with children and adults, and with normal clients, as well as with those having a variety of psychiatric problems (Bandura, 1969; Goldstein, 1973). Also, modeling can produce three general types of behavior change in the repertoire of the observer:

1. The observer can acquire new responses or patterns of behavior that he did not previously have.

2. Responses or behavior patterns that previously were performed by the observer but which have been suppressed by social disapproval or anxiety can be strengthened.

3. Previously performed behaviors, which have not been shown for a period of time, because of a depressed person's apathy or withdrawal, can be "released" or facilitated by observing a model display those behaviors.

People do not imitate all the myriad behaviors demonstrated to them in everyday life; rather, they *selectively* learn through observation. Applying modeling to Personal Effectiveness requires attention to certain procedures that can increase the likelihood that clients will selectively learn the behaviors which the counselor displays for them.

The client will carefully watch the model to determine if the performance is vivid and can be seen and heard easily. Therefore, choose models who you know can demonstrate the desired behavior; position the observer in a spot with unobstructed visibility for the model; remove or minimize extraneous noise and activities from the room. Attentiveness is also helped by the variation inherent in *multiple modeling,* i.e., where several models demonstrate their way of dealing with the situation in rapid succession. Stylistic variation of adequate performances provides a choice for the observing client at the same time that it rivets his attention on modeling. The model should have the following characteristics.

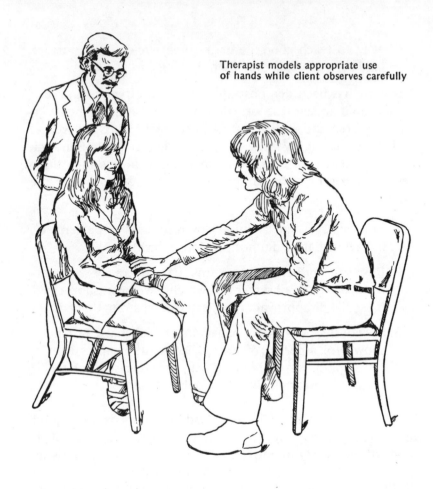

Therapist models appropriate use of hands while client observes carefully

1. *He should be similar in age, sex and other background characteristics to the observer.*

2. *He should be viewed as having high status, power and competence.* Therefore, the counselor selects models who are respected and admired by the client who is observing.

3. *He should be rewarded for engaging in the behavior being displayed.* Therefore, always give approval and recognition to the models for their efforts in Personal Effectiveness.

The observing client will be more likely to learn the behaviors being demonstrated by the model if the client is:

1. *Instructed clearly and specifically on the pertinent features of the model's behavior.* Therefore, the counselor always annotates and describes in advance the aspects of the model's performance that he especially wants the observer to follow. He can also narrate these features when the modeling is being performed.

2. *Overtly and covertly able to rehearse the modeled behavior immediately after it has been presented.* Therefore, the observing client should be brought back into the scene for a rerun as soon as the model has completed the demonstration, and should be asked to imagine himself behaving like the model.

3. *Rewarded for any approximation of the modeled behavior.* Therefore, the counselor provides incentives (approval, positive ratings, credits, tokens) to his clients when they improve their performance as a result of observing a model. Also, he has them anticipate receiving approval and positive feedback even before they try the rerun.

Below is a brief example of a counselor intervening to model a job interview scene for his client.

C: That was fine, Jim. I really think you did a good job of "selling yourself" because you made eye contact and had good voice volume. Let's work a little more on your posture and gestures. Let me run through the scene by taking your part. I'd like you to watch especially how I sit and lean forward at times to show interest, and also how I use my hands instead of keeping them crossed on my lap.

After the counselor models, the client rehearses the scene again. The steps for reviewing the training process for Personal Effectiveness are listed below.

1. A dry run for the purpose of assessment.

2. Modeling the behavior.

3. Having the client rerun the scene.

The counselor directs the client to the facets of his performance which were demonstrated by the model and which require improvement during the rerun.

> C: You just watched how Terry expressed tenderness by reaching out and touching the person role playing your wife. Now I'd like you to replay the scene and concentrate on leaning forward and touching your "wife" and at the same time to speak in a soft tone of voice. Your eye contact was terrific last time, so just keep that up.

During the replay the counselor uses prompts and positive feedback to help the participant make the desired improvements in his behavior. The rerun, like the dry run, should be focused on a specific behavioral goal and should be brief. Scenes can be as brief as 30 seconds but rarely should exceed 5 minutes. Information is given below to demonstrate the use of prompting and positive feedback for getting the improvement that clients want in their social behavior.

Prompting
Prompting is a means for bringing about a specific action by direct instructions, cues or signals given to the client during the rehearsal of a scene. This is done verbally or with sign language and can be done while a scene is in progress. The instructions that a counselor gives to a client at the start of the rerun are important for directing the performance toward a higher level of skill and effectiveness. The instructions should be brief. The counselor should avoid lecturing and giving moral lessons. The preparatory directions should focus on those one, two or three nonverbal components which have just been modeled for the client. Prompts given with incisive authoritativeness are particularly helpful in moving clients into action (especially new clients) who are reluctant to do or say anything, who may even be too inhibited to attempt

Role playing affection by leaning forward with eye contact and touching

imitating a modeled behavior. Even the most withdrawn and inhibited clients will respond by complying with a prompt, provided that the request is for a small and simple bit of verbal or nonverbal behavior. By reducing the "cost" of responding, the counselor spurs the client into a brief and successful rehearsal.

Prompting can also be employed while working on a more complex behavior by breaking the behavior down into its constituent components. The specific verbal content of an assertive skill may be prompted while several nonverbal aspects may be modeled, or perhaps broken down into more simple components and then each prompted in turn. For example, when working with a mother who is trying to get her child to pick up after himself, the verbal behavior may be prompted if the counselor says to the client "Tell him that you are annoyed with his sloppiness and that he can't go out to play until his room is neat." The client's nonverbal, assertive style can be modeled or broken down into simple components (eye contact, voice volume, gestures), each one prompted by the counselor.

Prompting as well as modeling can be used for both simple and complex verbal and nonverbal behavior. The cues a counselor gives to a client can take many forms, ranging from simple hand signals to elaborate "doubling" and use of remote control, electronic equipment. Some examples of prompts are given below:

Hand signals

1. Forefinger moving across the throat or palm outstretched at client.	Stop
2. Hands moving horizontally as if pulling taffy between them.	Slow down
3. One hand moving in a fast, tight circle.	Speed up
4. One, two, three or more fingers held up.	One, two, or more minutes remaining in the scene
5. Hands manipulating mouth in an exaggerated smile or frown.	Smile or look serious
6. Both palms up, moving up and down.	Talk louder
7. Both palms down, moving up and down.	Talk softer
8. Forefinger and thumb forming a circle, the other three fingers extended.*	Great job, good work, keep it up

* Do not use this last sign for people recently arrived from Mexico or people with a strong Mexican cultural affiliation. To us in the USA it signifies approval; to Mexicans it is an invitation to perform an unnatural act upon oneself.

Therapist gives hand signal to client, prompting louder voice

Doubling

The counselor hovers near the client, a little to the rear, playing the client's role in the scene with the other role player while the client merely listens and faces the other person. The counselor can gradually fade the doubling and encourage the client to take over in a step-wise fashion.

Verbal Prompts

The counselor gives either verbal instructions to the client or intervenes in a scene with brief verbal responses to be imitated. An elegant method for delivering verbal prompts is the "bug-in-the-ear device." This is a remote control, electronic device that allows the counselor to give verbal prompts and feedback privately to the client while a scene is going on. Without disturbing or interfering with the progress of interaction, the counselor can give prompts that only the client can hear through the ear plug. This enables the counselor to exert close control over the content of the client's speech and is particularly helpful when the client complains of being at a total loss about *what* to say. While the client is speaking, the counselor can give prompts such as, "Look at him!" or "Talk louder!" or "Your eye contact is good. Keep it up and use your hands." Bug-in-the-ear devices are commercially available (Farrell Instrument Company, Grand Island, Nebraska) or can be fabricated from a tape recorder, earplug, microphone and connecting wires. A portable, hand-held device, the Porta-Prompter, has been used successfully in family therapy and group sessions for Personal Effectiveness (Weathers and Liberman, 1973).

Below is an example of the use of prompts when a client practices asking a friend out for coffee.

Client: (Very softly) Hi, how have you been?

Counselor: (Gestures to client to talk louder)

Client: I was wondering, when . . . . (The client stops, looks bewildered and says he can't think of anything to say)

Counselor: (Moves next to client and whispers in his ear) It's really been a long time since I've seen you . . . .

Therapist whispers a prompt

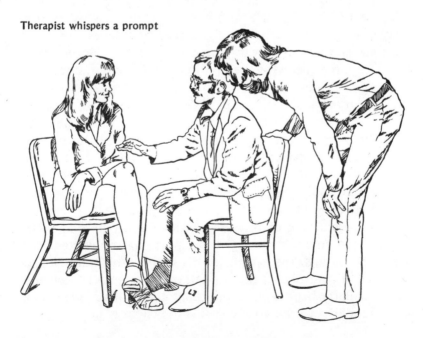

74

Client: It's really been a long time since I've seen you. We probably have a lot of things to talk over. How about taking a coffee break?

Counselor: Good!

Shaping

Shaping is the method of rewarding small improvements in a client's behavior. Limited goals are set for each session and small increments in performance are reinforced. Within each session, shaping is used to break the behavioral goal into small components. Thus, eye contact is worked on first before moving to gestures and voice volume. Each nonverbal and verbal component is successively trained until the total picture, or *gestalt*, is satisfactorily expressed. Similarly, the process of gaining increased Personal Effectiveness over a number of sessions can be viewed as a shaping procedure since successive goals are more difficult. The counselor does not target a new goal for training until the easier one is first attained.

A counselor should always have a "shaping attitude." He should never overlook even the slightest improvement and he should learn to recognize and favorably respond to behaviors that are bringing the client nearer to his ultimate goals. Social approval is given for each step or small gain. An effective shaper also makes sure that the client knows what is being rewarded. When giving feedback to a client on his performance, the counselor should be clear in his description of the behavior to be reinforced. For instance, he may intend to reward a client for speaking louder by merely saying "that was good." However, if the client is also not making eye contact, he may misunderstand what he did that was good and come to the wrong conclusion. The confusion can be avoided if the counselor says, "Your voice loudness was good."

Below is an example of a counselor (C) shaping a client who is learning to initiate conversations. The counselor rewards the client with smiles, nods, and praise for any behavior that brings him closer to his training goal.

C: Michelle, would you like to try striking up a conversation with Roger?

Michelle: OK.

C: Why don't you sit facing each other. Michelle, don't forget about your eye contact and the hand gestures that you did so well last session. Remember, too, that last time your voice was a little too soft. Go ahead now and try.

Michelle: (Looking down) Hi.

Roger: Hello.

Michelle: (Making eye contact)

C: (Nods)

Michelle: (A little softly) Umm, have you seen the paper today?

Roger: Yes, what do you think about the bank robbery?

Michelle: (Gesturing, speaking loudly enough, and making eye contact) You know, that was right down the street from where I live.

C: (Smiles and nods)

Roger: You don't say. How much did they get?

Michelle: (Gesturing with both hands like a baseball umpire signaling "safe," but avoiding eye contact) Not a thing!

C: Good gesture.

Roger: What happened?

Michelle: (Gesturing, leaning forward, but with infrequent eye contact) The alarm went off and the robbers panicked.

C: OK, very good, Michelle, especially your gestures and posture. Your voice was a little too soft at the beginning, but it picked up fine.

Specific examples of the shaping of stepwise behavioral goals over successive sessions of Personal Effectiveness are given in Table 3, page 78.

Positive Feedback

Throughout the course of a scene positive feedback in the form of praise, applause, and pats-on-the-back is used to let the client know how well he has performed. Often behavior can be rewarded without interrupting a scene by merely nodding the head, saying "mm-hmm," "good," or smiling. Any of these will tell the client that he has just done something right. Various verbal and nonverbal indicators of approval are powerful ways to strengthen appropriate, desirable behavior in your clients. When approval or positive feedback increases the frequency of desirable behavior, it is called *social reinforcement*. Social reinforcers, sometimes called "socials" or "warm-fuzzies," motivate the client to stay on the same track or to repeat what he's just done. If at all possible, social reinforcement should immediately follow the behavior that is being rewarded. The beneficial effect is most powerful when praise is given during and immediately after the behavioral rehearsal. Immediate reinforcement or feedback makes it easy for the client to know what he is doing well. Positive feedback is an important feature of shaping human behavior. Shaping means that frequent approval is given for successively better attempts. Any sign of improvement is clearly, immediately and specifically praised. Social rewards are the most effective types of reinforcers for people. In addition, they don't cost anything, are always available, and can be closely tailored to the client's needs and values.

Each time someone rehearses in Personal Effectiveness the counselor has an opportunity to strengthen desirable behavior with praise. As a leader of Personal Effectiveness the counselor must be sensitive to any and all signs of improvement and be ready to interject positively. After every scene, other group members focus on the specific things that the participant did better. For example, a counselor might ask the group, "Who can give John some feedback on the way he reached out to shake hands in that scene?" He can induce

Table 3 Shaping Progressive Behavioral Goals

Case 1: Conversational Skills

1. Start a conversation with staff member at lunch.
2. Start a conversation with two new clients at day treatment center.
3. Discuss the day's activities at day treatment center with boarding home operator for a five-minute period.
4. Go to a restaurant and engage waitress in a conversation for three minutes about the quality of the food.
5. Start a conversation about the weather with a fellow passenger on the city bus on the way to the clinic.

Case 2: Job Seeking Skills

1. Call two friends and ask if they know of any job opportunities.
2. Go to state employment office and ask for leads for jobs.
3. Go to local supermarket or department store and ask for an application form.
4. Return completed application form to the store and ask for an interview.
5. Go for an interview.
6. Return to the store to let the manager know that you are still interested.

Case 3: Asserting Oneself at Home With the Family

1. Tell children to not be so loud during dinner.
2. Talk with wife (husband) about chores he/she has neglected.
3. Tell children they can't have bikes for Christmas because of the expense.
4. Take the lead role in planning a family picnic at the beach.
5. Make plans for a weekend trip with the entire family.

Case 4: Getting A Date

1. Ask a co-ed in class if you can review her notes from the last class.
2. Have a conversation with her after class in which you exchange three pieces of personal information with her; e.g., how long she has gone to that school, where she lives, why she does or does not like the class, her interests outside of school, her career plans, etc.
3. Ask her to join you for coffee at the student union.
4. Ask her if she would like to hear the "terrific new band," or see the "great new movie" that is playing in town.

positive thinking and evaluating in his group by modeling liberal, positive feedback, and by cutting off criticism and negative confrontation. See Figure 5, page 80.

Important! The counselor cannot give a person *too much* positive feedback. Profusely seeding improved behavior with approval will yield a bumper harvest in Personal Effectiveness.

In the last example the counselor (C) provided social reinforcement by nodding his head, smiling, and saying "good." Below is another example of a counselor shaping desirable behavior by providing positive feedback. This client is a young man, Louis, rehearsing a job interview.

C: Louis, let's try that job interview again today. Who would you like to work with?

Louis: Joe.

C: OK, Joe, would you pretend you're interviewing Louis for a job as a grocery clerk? Just ask him a few questions about his previous experience and ability.

Joe: Sure.

C: Louis, remember to smile, show interest, and be confident. Don't be afraid to talk about yourself and be sure to use gestures to show you're interested. OK? Go ahead, Joe.

Joe: Well, Louis, I see on your application that you worked in a store once before. How did you like it?

Louis: (No gestures) It was OK.

Joe: Can you tell me what you did?

Louis: (No gestures) I sold shoes.

Joe: Did you get along well with the customers?

Louis: (Relaxing, smiling, gesturing confidently) Oh, yes, I enjoyed talking to them and a lot of them would come back again and ask for me.

C: (Nodding) Good.

Figure 5   Flow Chart Depicting the Remediation of Social Skills in the Training Session

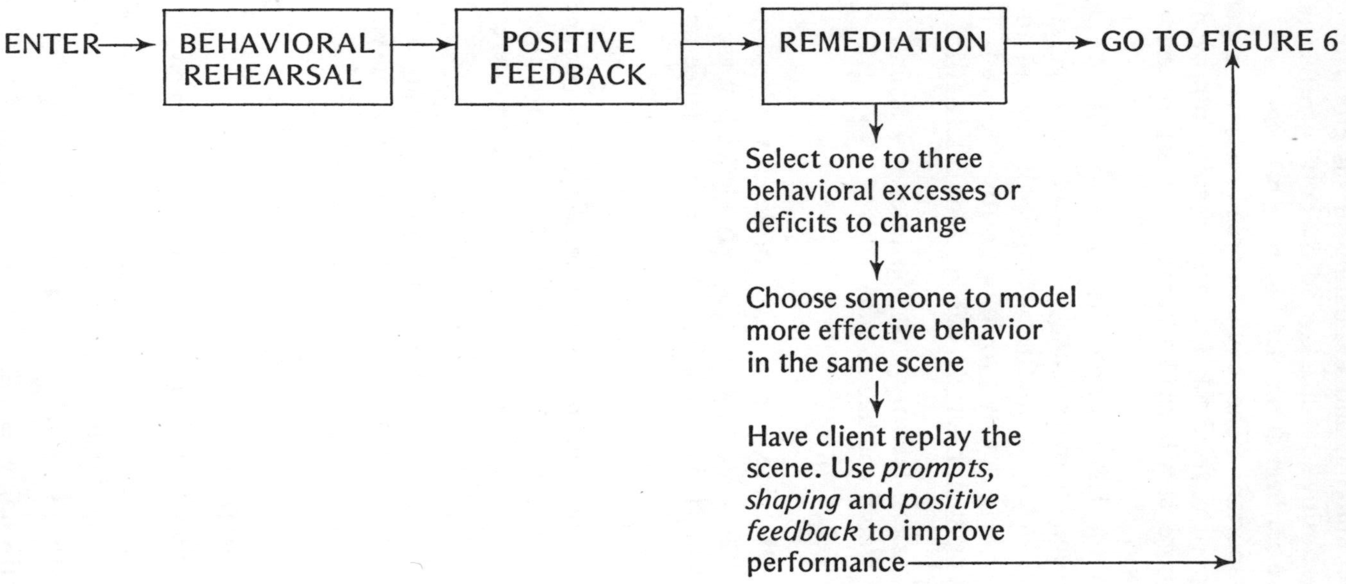

ENTER → BEHAVIORAL REHEARSAL → POSITIVE FEEDBACK → REMEDIATION → GO TO FIGURE 6

Under REMEDIATION:

Select one to three behavioral excesses or deficits to change

↓

Choose someone to model more effective behavior in the same scene

↓

Have client replay the scene. Use *prompts*, *shaping* and *positive feedback* to improve performance

Joe: Did you make a lot of sales?

Louis: (Leaning forward and gesturing) Let me tell you, I was number one salesman five of the six months I worked there.

C: Good posture and gestures, Louis. You're doing fine.

Joe: Well, do you think you could do as well in a grocery?

Louis: (Making solid eye contact and gesturing) I'm sure of it. I've always wanted to work in a grocery store and I know I'll do a good job for you.

C: Excellent, especially the eye contact. You're hired, Louis.

In addition to verbal feedback given during and after scenes, numerical ratings, points, tokens or credits which are redeemable for tangible rewards, or other symbolic incentives can be given to participants for their efforts and improvements. Each performance is rated on eye contact, facial expression, gestures, posture, voice tone, voice loudness, speech fluency, speech content and choice of words (see chart, page 82).

At the Oxnard Mental Health Center a structured format has been devised to promote systematic feedback for behavioral rehearsals in group sessions of Personal Effectiveness. A rating system, based on the judging of diving and gymnastic events, is used. Four or more group members are asked to rate a series of scenes on a 1 to 5 scale. The scale is relative and each participant is rated in comparison to his previous performance rather than in comparison to others in the group. Thus, each person competes with his own behavioral rehearsals. The ratings are anchored by the following guidelines:

1 = Very poor; desirable behavior is lacking.

2 = Fair; needs much improvement.

3 = Average; can still stand improvement.

4 = Good; needs only refinement and polishing.

5 = Excellent; little or no room for improvement.

A blackboard is set up and outlined as follows:

	Judge			
	A	B	C	D
Facial Expression				
Use of Hands			•	
Voice Loudness				
Posture				
Eye Contact				
Voice Tone				
Fluency				
Content				

All those present, clients and staff alike, raise from one to five fingers to indicate their assessment of the performance. A group member who has been assigned the job of recording the "average" rating on the blackboard "eyeballs" the assessments, roughly approximates the average, and writes it on the board. High ratings are accompanied by verbal praise from clients and staff, while low ratings are accompanied by encouragement for improvement next time. The counselor randomly selects members to explain and document their ratings, especially high ratings. For example, "Jack, why did you give Laura a rating of '5' for facial expression?" By asking clients to explain their ratings, participation and involvement among members is increased. Group cohesiveness is also enhanced because clients feel that they are helping each other.

Members of the group who deviate markedly from the average rating are asked to explain their ratings. For example, the counselor asks the following question, "Jeanne, your rating was a little lower than the others. I wonder if you could tell us why you gave Mickey a rating of '2' on posture? How could he have earned a '4'?" The explanation is then followed by discussion until the discrepancy is resolved. For highly rated performances the counselor may choose to award tokens or points which can be exchanged for material rewards.

It should be emphasized that the 5-point scale is adapted to each client; it is not an absolute scale. The client's

Group members rate client who has just completed a behavioral rehearsal

initial level of ability and length of time in Personal Effectiveness are considered. In addition, generosity is always the rule: the ratings should "bend" toward "giving" positive feedback. In addition to these public ratings, one counselor or co-leader records his own ratings for all clients on the Personal Effectiveness Record Sheet (Appendix, page 144).

Formal or semistructured rating systems have a side benefit beyond the massive, group feedback they engender for participants going through behavioral rehearsals. These systems evoke a high level of active involvement by group members in each other's efforts to improve their social skills. Since each person may be called upon to document his rating of another participant, no one can afford to sit back and ignore the group proceedings. Even withdrawn or self-preoccupied clients tend to sit at the edge of their chairs and carefully monitor the behavioral rehearsals of the other group members. Cohesiveness is promoted as group members learn more about each other, "tune-in" to each other's progress, and provide tangible help to one another. Learning new ways to express emotions and make social contact through *modeling* are enhanced because the participants in the group must pay closer attention to each other's performances in order to give informed ratings. The counselor can shape attending on the part of isolated and withdrawn members by prompting their evaluations and then granting them approval for their verbal feedback. The member who monitors the blackboard ratings can improve his own verbal and nonverbal skills while soliciting and summarizing feedback from the group (see Figure 6).

Tricks for Treatment

Before beginning the long and sometimes frustrating endeavor as a trainer of Personal Effectiveness, the counselor should read some useful exercises, below, that will help clients and students express their feelings more assertively. We have collected these exercises from a variety of sources, but we encourage the invention of others.

Speak a Little Louder!

The counselor instructs the client to stand ten to twenty feet away from him or another participant and to replay the scene at that distance. The purpose of this exercise is to prompt clients who are quiet and soft-spoken, or who mumble to speak louder. Sometimes it may be necessary to have the client actually stand outside the room or by the doorway. He is discharged from the behavioral rehearsal only after

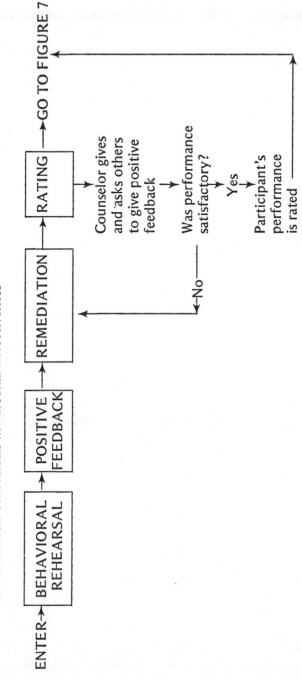

Figure 6   Flow Chart Depicting the Use of Group Ratings to Enhance Positive Feedback on the Replay of Behavioral Rehearsals in Personal Effectiveness

ENTER→ BEHAVIORAL REHEARSAL → POSITIVE FEEDBACK → REMEDIATION → RATING →GO TO FIGURE 7

Counselor gives and asks others to give positive feedback

Was performance satisfactory?

—No—

Yes

Participant's performance is rated

he satisfactorily increases voice volume and can be heard by the counselor and the interpersonal target across the room. When the appropriately loud speech is heard, the counselor and the other group members reinforce it with positive feedback. Initially, the client may have to shout from across the room to be heard clearly, but the vocal response can gradually be shaped to fit social expectations by having him slowly move closer to the person he is addressing.

This exercise is good practice for people who mumble. Besides role playing real-life scenes, clients can simply practice giving information about themselves. For example, the counselor might say something like the following:

> Jerry, I'd like you to stand in the doorway on the other side of the room and tell me as many things about your car as you can. Describe the car to me and tell me about the problems you have with it. This will help you learn to speak more loudly and clearly. When I can't hear you, I'll raise my arms and you'll have to speak up. OK?

Another way to increase voice volume is to use an electronic device called a "Voice Light" or a voice-activated relay. A microphone located at a selected distance from the client picks up his sounds and, if the sound is loud enough, a preset switch closes and a light goes on or a needle is deflected on a dial. By making the light or dial visible to the client as well as the counselor, positive feedback is provided in an ongoing fashion as the client carries on a conversation. The "Voice Light" is especially helpful for people who have been secluded or institutionalized for long periods, and who have engaged in very little meaningful conversation on a daily basis. Increasing voice loudness is often one of the first steps in the shaping of conversational skills, assertiveness, and other more complex social and emotional behaviors.

Tonal Exercises
Tone of voice communicates tension, fear, anger, tenderness, as well as assertiveness. Since voice tone is controlled by breathing mechanisms (the relaxation and contraction of

respiratory and throat muscles), exercises can assist a person to get into normal ranges of pitch.

1. To develop proper resonance in your chest, keep your hand on your chest bones (ribs and sternum) just under the collar bone and feel them vibrating as you talk. Make sure your teeth are separated enough to let the sound come out. To find your optimum pitch, place your hand on your chest, lower your voice a half tone at a time while repeating, "I don't think it's going to rain." When you get uncomfortable at the very low tones, stop and go up one tone which will be close to your optimum pitch.

2. To relax the throat muscles, change your tongue position by alternately pressing your tongue against the roof of your mouth and then relaxing it. Do the same contraction and relaxation exercise with the muscles of your jaws. Use chewing motions to help relieve over-straining the throat area. Yawning and sighing also help to stretch and relax.

3. To relax chest and diaphragm muscles, use deep breathing exercises and alternately contract and relax these muscles by inhaling deeply, holding your breath, and then slowly and fully exhaling. Energize your voice by sitting with your chest up and out and your solar plexis contracted and pulled in toward the spine. Maintain this position as you speak.

Silent Movie Gambit
When a person displays stiff and frozen facial expressions, gestures, and posture, the counselor can have him pretend that he is in a silent movie in order to do exercises that evoke nonverbal expression of emotion. The counselor instructs the client to play a scene in which he is to express emotion (joy, annoyance, love, firmness) without speaking. The client moves his lips as if speaking, but his task is to convey emotion primarily with his hands, facial expression, and body posture. For example, he may rehearse a scene where he is

confronted by an inconsiderate roommate. He would then display anger and assertiveness without using words. The client puts his hands on his hips, makes intensive eye contact, points his finger while moving his lips, and perhaps hits his right fist into his left palm for emphasis. This exercise demands exaggerated use of these nonverbal aspects of communication and helps rectify the student's "wooden" appearance.

Positive Statements

The "Downshouter" is an appropriate name that the Irish have for someone who doesn't have a good word for anyone or anything. We all know people who see the bleak, discouraging, and pessimistic side of every topic of conversation. It's easy to find yourself going along with the "Downshouter," getting glummer yourself as one negative comment and reaction leads to another. Because overt behavior can influence feelings and attitudes, rehearsing positive statements can help to change the mood of people who are depressed, cynical, or negative. The client is asked to talk about something without being critical or without complaining. In some cases a topic is provided, e.g., politics, the economy, weather, or sports. Feedback is withheld until the end of the scene unless the client lapses into negative statements; if he does, the counselor intervenes, gives approval for positive verbalizations, points out the negative statements, and instructs the client to try again. Below is an example of the "positive statements" exercise:

> C: Glenn, you seem to be "down" today, so I think it would be a good idea to work on developing a more positive attitude. I'd like to see how long you can go making only positive statements and reactions about a really bad problem—the high price of gasoline. I'll complain to you about the high cost of gas and then you try to convince me that there are good sides to it—how it will decrease pollution, save lives from traffic deaths, and so on. OK, shall we start?

Glenn: I'll try.

C: Good.

. I think these gas prices are ridiculous; I just don't think it's fair that we have to be paying so much for gas. How do you feel about it?

Glenn: Well, the prices are sort of high, but I'm sure the oil companies have some very good reasons.

C: I don't think so; I think we're being robbed and I'm sick of it.

Glenn: I guess you're right.

C: Hold it. Remember, Glenn, you're supposed to be totally positive and you just agreed with me that we're being robbed. Let's try again.

I think we're being robbed and I'm sick of it.

Glenn: It may just seem like we're paying too much because we've always had it so good. Our prices are still much lower than gas prices in Europe.

C: What about the shortages? You can't even get enough gas.

Glenn: Maybe this will help us to conserve gas and people will be less wasteful. It may turn out to be a good thing in the long run.

C: Nice going, Glenn. You almost had me convinced. You can be very persuasive. I think we should do more of this tomorrow. Also, I'd like you to find some time to talk to one of the nurses and tell her in a positive way how much better you are doing this week. Make sure she initials your Personal Effectiveness assignment card. Bring the card with you to the Planning Meeting tomorrow.

Video Tape Feedback
Video tape is an extremely effective method for maintaining involvement and active participation in groups. However, in most settings it is somewhat cumbersome and requires more time be spent with each client if it is to produce the maxi-

mum effect. Video feedback should be used within the following guidelines:

1. *Tape short scenes;* 2 minutes is too long, 30 seconds is about right.

2. *Provide feedback* after each scene.

3. *Use stop action,* if possible, to highlight examples of *good* aspects of performing facial expression, posture, eye contact, and gestures.

4. *Focus on improved performance.* Do not focus on examples of poor performance. This is very tempting because the mistakes people make are so obvious on video tape. *Resist the urge to "freeze" the picture on especially inept actions.*

While video feedback is very graphic in its display of both verbal and nonverbal segments of behavior, it is expensive and requires careful handling to keep it functioning properly, and an additional person to use the camera. More economical, but also effective, is the use of a large mirror to reflect nonverbal behavior to the participants in behavioral rehearsals. Facial animation is very important in communicating meaning; to be deadpan is like wearing a mask. A counselor or another group member can hold the mirror in front of the person practicing a scene to provide ongoing feedback on facial expression, posture, and use of hands. Some clients can be instructed to keep a mirror near their home telephone so that they can see their facial expressions while talking.

Broken Record

Many clients have trouble deciding how to defend their rights in an encounter with someone else. They often feel they must come up with something new in response to everything said by the other person. This, however, only leads to a cycle of defensiveness and apology or anger. One way to prevent exploitation by others is the broken record technique. This technique removes the pressure of coming up with something new to say every time the client engages in conversation. The client is simply asked to repeat his position statement over and over as if he were a broken record. This is often used when helping a client say "No" to someone. He may desire to decline an offer to buy encyclopedias, used cars, or pots and pans, or he may simply want to refuse an unreasonable request from a friend or family member. The counselor has the client say, without apology, "No! I'm not interested in doing that." "No! I'm not interested in doing that." "No! I'm not interested in doing that." The client makes the refusal statement, allows the other role player to come back with a variation of the request, and then repeats his refusal. The broken record technique is especially helpful for clients who have a hard time saying no without giving an elaborate excuse or justification. This procedure teaches the client that he can say no without going into a long explanation of why simply because he feels the request is unreasonable.

The other way to use the broken record procedure is for the counselor to have a client make a request of someone. Once again he does not have to come up with a new request or elaboration to every response by the other person. The client can say, "It is really important to me and I would really appreciate your doing it." As the other person offers excuses, the client repeats the same line.

Fogging

Another procedure used to help the client decline unreasonable requests is called fogging. The client uses the therapeutic technique of reflecting back to the other person what he has just said, and then adding, "But I'm sorry, I just can't do that." Someone asks the client if he can borrow the client's car for the evening because it is very important that he make a doctor's appointment and he has no transportation. The client's fogging response would be, "Gee, I know how important it is to you that you get to the doctor's office tonight, and how lost you feel without any transportation to get there, *but* I'm sorry I can't lend you my car tonight." Another way is to have someone try to get a client to go along on a social outing that he doesn't care to attend.

The dialogue would be something like, "Bill, I've got two tickets for the ballgame tonight and it's only two hours away and there is nobody I would like to go with me more than you. Can you put everything down and get ready to go?" Bill might say, "I know how excited you are about getting the tickets and I know how much you want me to go, but I'm sorry I can't tonight." The fogging technique allows the clients to give feedback to the other person about their own feelings while saying no. It fogs the situation rather than giving "No" straight out or going into a long explanation. Fogging also communicates an emphatic response to the other person which softens the impact of the "No."

Sell Me Something
Many clients have words that they want to say, but have trouble saying them without engaging in filler sounds (e.g., "Uh, you know") as they talk. This has to do with the non-verbal variable of fluency. The exercise known as "sell me something" can help increase a client's fluency. The client chooses something that he would like to sell to someone else; he tries to give a one-minute sales presentation without engaging in any filler sounds. The first time through the client may have difficulty, but by the second or third rehearsal he should show improvement. The idea is not to make salesmen out of the clients, but to give them a concrete exercise in which they can increase their fluency while talking to other people.

The Executive Session
In many intimate relationships communication is a serious problem that is often caused by one of the persons not taking time to listen closely to the other person. The "Executive Session" is a Personal Effectiveness technique that calls for one person to speak; the second person then gives feedback to the first person about what it is that he said. The second person has to give feedback about the first person's message that indicates that the message being sent was clear. When the first person agrees that the second person understood the message that was being sent, then and only then can the second person

"send" a message to the first person. The first person then repeats the message to the second person's satisfaction and so forth. This technique slows down the communication process and often reduces the highly charged emotional characteristics of conversations between intimate persons. An example of this is a husband (H) and wife (W) talking about a budgeting problem. Husband, "I don't understand why you can't balance the checkbook every month so that we're not overdrawn at the bank all the time." Wife, "I hear you saying that you're upset that I don't balance the checkbook, and that you would like that to change." Husband, "Yes, that's right." Wife, "I want to say that I would like you to take the responsibility of balancing the checkbook and doing the budget so that you can know the problems in meeting our budget." Husband, "Well, I hear you saying that you want me to take on this responsibility of budgeting and handling the checkbook, is that right?" Wife, "Yes!" The Executive Session can help a couple build empathy and mutual understanding since it can be used at home as well as in the training or treatment setting.

Overcoming Resistance to Role Playing
One of the more difficult things to do in the Personal Effectiveness training is to get a new, resistant client to role play. This section will describe some of the procedures that we have found to be effective in overcoming this resistance.

1. To reduce resistance to role playing, the counselor begins the session with the most enthusiastic clients. He then proceeds to the clients who may be more resistant. In this way momentum of the group is built up and the counselor has an opportunity to call on the resistant clients to give feedback to those who are participating. This procedure gets the resistant client involved in talking and participating in the group, if only for feedback.

2. In the same vein, if the counselor suspects that a client is resistant to role playing a scene of his own, he can ask that client to take on the role of spouse, employer, or friend in the role play scene with another client. After

this experience, it should be easier for the clients to role play their own scene.

3. Once the counselor discovers a resistant client, a good thing to do is to sincerely acknowledge the client's stated reasons for being reluctant to role play. For example, if the client says that a role play situation is not a real-life situation and is artificial, the counselor can add that it is still helpful for the client to increase his skills as well as permitting an assessment of what he is doing well that does not need improvement.

4. Another procedure is to get the resistant client "to try a short scene"; this may be no more than introducing himself to three people in the room and telling them what his home state is and then asking two others where they were born and raised. Often a short scene is the most that can be expected from resistant clients. Later they will become more comfortable with the counselor, the other people in the group, and the group format.

5. Another procedure is to call on a veteran member of the group to talk about how he felt when he first tried to role play. The counselor asks the veteran client to explain how different he feels after going through many role playing experiences.

These procedures are merely ways to overcome resistance to role playing. Obviously at no time should clients be coerced or pushed into a role play experience if they strongly feel that they do not want to participate. Clients can assertively say that they do not want to participate and their rights must be respected.

Practice Exercise 2

Using the "clients" described on page 10 of the Planning Meeting, try the training techniques we have described. Pair off, take turns role playing the client and counselor, rehearse brief scenes, and discuss your performances. Remember, work with limited goals, have a "shaping attitude," and be explicit and generous when providing positive feedback. Although more than one technique should be used on any client, we suggest that you choose *one* training technique to concentrate on for each person. Remember that *modeling* is especially effective with new clients, with complex behaviors, and with nonverbal behaviors; *prompting* is effective with inhibited clients, with simple behaviors and with verbal behaviors. In the Training Session, you as a "counselor" may also want to try the techniques with "clients" and problem situations you make up yourself.

Strategies for Intervention

Although the counselor can decide which training technique to apply to a particular client before beginning a scene, during the course of a scene he may have to spontaneously employ other techniques to attain the desired behavioral goals. After having modeled for a client, the counselor may find it necessary to prompt him toward successful imitation. He must also decide when to cut scenes short because the client is off the track, floundering, becoming anxious, upset, or displaying undesirable behaviors. Continuing the practice under these conditions may have a negative effect.

Experienced counselors do these things smoothly, intuitively and spontaneously, hardly aware of what prompts their intervention. Furthermore, different counselors have different styles and no one strategy covers them all. However, we can suggest some general guidelines for intervention. The usual interventions are modeling, instructions, prompting, giving positive feedback, and ending a scene. The client's behavior that normally precedes and cues each of these interventions will be delineated. In this section we attempt to help the counselor who finds himself in the midst of a scene asking, "What do I do now?"

When to Model
Modeling is usually employed when verbal instructions or a

simple prompt would not be effective for the following reasons:

1. The client is not giving any response.

2. He does not understand what to do or, perhaps, is not able to perform.

3. He is performing well except for nonverbal, emotional behavior.

Modeling is often introduced by saying something like, "Let me give you some idea of what I mean." The intervention is normally prompted by the client's failure to follow directions to rehearse a scene, or an inappropriate behavioral perform-ance *and* a high probability that instructions or prompting would not be sufficient to evoke the desired behavior. While modeling is effective in teaching a new repertoire of responses, the client should have the basic elements of the responses in his existing repertoire.

When to Prompt

A counselor usually prompts for the following reasons:

1. The client is giving some response and seems to be on the right track.

2. He is deficient in one or two *simple* nonverbal behaviors such as smiling, or eye contact as opposed to an overall lack of many emotionally expressive behaviors.

3. He is deficient in some relatively simple verbal behavior.

A prompt is a nudge in a specific direction, so it helps if the client is already "leaning" in that direction. In contrast, modeling is more an example than a nudge. The more complex or varied the possible responses, the less likely it is that prompting will be effective. A prompt is usually given when the client is providing the counselor with some behav-ior to work with and the counselor has a good idea of what, specifically, he wants the client to do. Prompting is often helpful when a client is trying to imitate behavior that the counselor has just modeled.

When to Give Positive Feedback
Positive feedback or social reinforcement should be provided when the client has performed well and when the feedback will not interrupt the scene. It is usually better to wait until the end of a scene to reward the client than to possibly distract him. However, there are a few exceptions to this:

1. A client who seems to be unsure of himself and probably needs some encouragement to carry him through the entire scene should be reinforced often during the action.

2. A client who has repeatedly attempted some behavior and finally gets it right should be reinforced immediately.

3. Some types of nonverbal positive feedback can be provided without causing interruption in the flow of the situation; for example, smiling, nodding the head or a "V" finger signal.

When to End a Scene
Some scenes have a natural ending; for example, scenes that involve asking for instructions, or asking someone out on a date. Other scenes are open-ended and must be terminated by the counselor. A few situations which may prompt the decision to end the scene are given below:

1. The scene seems to be too difficult for the client and no progress is being made.

2. The client is becoming increasingly anxious as evidenced by verbal dysfluencies, muscular tension, or a pained facial expression.

3. The client has successfully rehearsed the scene and additional performance would be superfluous.

Below is an example of a counselor using several behavioral techniques. Notice what sort of behavior on the part of the client causes the counselor (C) to implement the various techniques.

C: Chuck, you were going to practice initiating a conversation with a girl you'd like to ask out. Why don't you and Marcia work on that.

Chuck: I'm not sure how to start.

C: OK, let me give you an idea. (The counselor takes Chuck's seat and begins talking to Marcia, using gestures, smiling, and leaning forward at times to show interest.) Hello, my name is Chuck. What's yours?

Marcia: I'm Marcia.

C: Nice to meet you, Marcia. Do you live in the building, too?

Marcia: Yes, I moved in down the hall last week.

C: Hey that's great. What do you think of the place?

Marcia: It seems OK, but I really haven't met many people here yet.

C: I think you'll really like it. There are a lot of nice people, not much noise, and a good party once in a while. Say, Marcia, I was just on my way to lunch. Have you eaten yet?

Marcia: No, I haven't.

C: Would you like to join me?

Marcia: Yes, I'd like to.

C: OK. Now you try it, Chuck. Just relax and introduce yourself and start talking about something as I did.

Chuck: Hi, I'm Chuck. What's your name?

Marcia: I'm Marcia.

Chuck: Umm . . . . (Pause)

C: (Whispers to Chuck, "Have you been living around here long?")

Chuck: Have you been around here long?

     C: ("Good." Softly)

Marcia: No, I just moved in last week.

Chuck: (Softly) Oh, I wondered why I hadn't seen you too much.

     C: (Gestures to Chuck to talk more loudly.)

Chuck: How do you like your neighbors?

Marcia: Well, I really haven't met anyone yet, except you.

Chuck: Oh . . . . (Pause)

     C: (Whispers to Chuck, "Ask her if she's eaten lunch.")

Chuck: Have you eaten lunch yet today?

Marcia: No, I haven't.

Chuck: Would you like to come with me for lunch?

Marcia: Where are you going?

Chuck: I thought we could go out for a hamburger and maybe some ice cream.

     C: (Whispers to Chuck, "Good." Flashes "V" signal)

Marcia: That sounds fine. I'll get my coat.

Chuck: I'll come over to get you. What did you say your apartment was?

Marcia: Fifteen.

     C: Very good, Chuck. We'll stop here. Let's give Chuck some feedback on how he did, especially his eye contact and tone of voice.

Practice Exercise 3

Again using the clients on page 10, or those you've made up, pair off, role play the client and counselor, and try using all of the training techniques described. After each performance, discuss the techniques you used and what prompted you to implement them. Consider the following:

1. What was the client's initial level of ability?

2. Which behavior needed to be worked on (verbal, nonverbal, simple, complex)?

3. Was the client on the right track?

4. Was the client's overall communication style in need of change?

5. Would a simple verbal or nonverbal prompt have facilitated the scene?

6. Would some positive feedback have been helpful during the action or would it have been intrusive?

7. If the client faltered, would a nudge have been enough to get him going or was modeling necessary?

8. Was the client too anxious to go on?

9. Had the client accomplished enough so that the scene could have been terminated?

If you feel you've used any technique inappropriately, reread the relevant section of the manual, and rehearse the scene again.

Giving Real-Life Assignments

Real-life assignments to carry out the social and emotional behaviors rehearsed in the Training Session are a critically important facet of Personal Effectiveness. Unless a person actually performs the behavior that he practiced in the Training Session in a real-life situation, no progress can be said to have occurred. Family, job, school, and community situations are the crucibles within which Personal Effectiveness is tested. Training cannot be viewed as successful until the participant's behavioral goals are generalized, transferred, and realized outside of the training site. Assignments are an intrinsic part of the Personal Effectiveness procedure. The results of these assignments are the best measure of the effectiveness of training.

As the counselor gives behavioral assignments in Personal Effectiveness, he maximizes the chances of success and minimizes the possibility of failure. Success and progress can be promoted by adjusting the required assignments to the abilities and readiness of the client. By making the assignment easy enough to accomplish, a successful experience is ensured. Each successfully completed assignment serves as a natural reinforcer for further progress and efforts; it also strengthens self-confidence. The degree of difficulty of assignments can be gradually increased as success occurs with easier or more simple goals. The counselor determines appropriate types of goals and assignments with a new client by observing behavioral assets and limitations displayed during the Training Session and during other social interactions. The counselor also uses the experiences and history reported by the client and any relevant family members or friends. As time passes, the client's success or failure in completing assignments will serve as the counselor's most reliable guide to revising performance objectives and making new assignments. The counselor encourages clients to participate actively when choosing assignments to insure that they choose activities that have personal relevance.

Just as the clients reported on their previous real-life assignments in the Planning Meeting, the next assignment should be described in specific detail. In this way both client and counselor develop similar behavioral expectations. Success or failure can then be clearly defined and progress can be closely monitored. These assignments represent the true goals of Personal Effectiveness since behavioral changes in real life, not just in the treatment setting, represent the end points of training.

Because the real-life assignments correspond to scenes practiced in training, the criteria for a good assignment are the same as for the choice of scenes (see pages 36-38 of The Planning Meeting). Assignments should be positive, functional, and should deal with high frequency behaviors that occur naturally and regularly in the client's daily life. The choice of assignments over time is determined by his reports of progress and the counselor's estimation of the appropriate rate of treatment progress for a particular person. This rate will more than likely become evident during the first few sessions. Sometimes the counselor will gradually "shape" clients by repeating assignments several times and increasing their difficulty by very small increments. However, even for "faster" clients, the counselor should take care to avoid failures. A good rule of thumb is to "start where the client is" and then "let the client be the guide." The following lists of *successive goals* for clients, treated recently at the Day Treatment Center of the Oxnard Mental Health Center, illustrate the shaping aspects of Personal Effectiveness.

Case 1

1. Speak in a workshop.

2. Read in a group.

3. Talk about himself in a group.

4. Call the city council for the time of their next meeting.

5. Go to a city council meeting for one-half hour.

6. Go to a city council meeting and introduce himself.

Case 2

1. Initiate a conversation with another client at the Center.

2. Talk to staff about going to the beach over the weekend.

3. Introduce herself and get involved in a conversation at her yoga class.

4. Talk with her mother about positive things at the clinic and with her life.

5. Be interviewed for an electronics assembly workshop.

6. Talk with someone at the clinic who responds negatively.

7. Be interviewed for a volunteer job at a hospital.

Case 3

1. Talk to one person, find out three things about the person, and offer three pieces of information about himself.

2. Talk to friends who are overly concerned about his wife's death. Express appreciation for the concern and then get on to the present.

3. Talk to two new women. Introduce himself and have a conversation emphasizing positive statements.

4. Talk to someone about a football game he saw the previous night and practice voice volume.

5. Note interesting and positive things he does on vacation so he can tell the group when he returns.

6. Call a friend he hasn't seen in a long time and ask him to visit.

7. Answer calls about his job and arrange to do later work.

Case 4

1. Have a conversation with a staff member.

2. Talk with the pastor at church.

3. Meet company who visits the family at home.

4. Buy a cake pan in a store.

5. Get a library card.

6. Return a book to the library, pay a fine, and get a new book.

7. Introduce himself to a new neighbor.

8. Introduce himself to one new person and get personal information from him or her.

9. Go to the library and ask for a particular book.

10. Go to a community center and get a schedule of activities.

11. Talk to the landlady about having some work done.

Behavioral goals may focus on any of the interpersonal situations which arise in the client's life. Goals of recent clients participating in Personal Effectiveness include the following:

1. Talk with a neighbor without letting her "cry on your shoulder."

2. Approach three familiar people and say "Hello, how are you?"

3. Ask a sales clerk to help find an item.

4. Tell your son that he can't have a new bike for Christmas.

5. Get a job application.

6. Talk with your wife about taking over chores that she's neglected.

7. Cut off conversations with people who won't stop talking about negative things.

8. Have a positive conversation with someone who is depressed.

9. Say "No" to an invitation to play poker for high stakes.

10. Talk with your husband about problems.

11. Talk with your husband about having time alone.

One method of categorizing Personal Effectiveness goals is given in the Appendix (p. 146). It is by no means exhaustive, but it does indicate the range of possible behavioral goals

Therapist gives assignment on cue card to client who is to complete in the real world what he has just practiced

given as assignments within the organized framework of training.

Below are three illustrations of real-life assignments following success, failure, and repeated failure.

Success

C: Eddie, since you did so well last week talking to strangers, I think you could try something a little more difficult for this week. Is there anyone you've been having problems with or anyone you'd like to get to know better?

Eddie: Yes, there is a girl in one of my classes who I'd like to take out some weekend, but I'm not sure how to go about it.

C: I think we can work on that. Why don't we practice asking her to lunch at school before asking her out on a regular date. Your assignment for next week will be to ask her to lunch.

Notice how the counselor (C) allowed for progress by encouraging a more difficult goal but suggested a less difficult assignment (a lunch date) than the client mentioned (a date over the weekend).

Failure

C: Ann, since you had some difficulty getting your roommate to wash her dishes, I think perhaps we ought to work on this again. You've been making fine progress and I think you can do this assignment successfully if we work on it again today and go over the difficulties that you mentioned.

Ann: I think if I hadn't given up so easily when she got angry I could have done it.

C: Well, then, today we can have someone role play your roommate and have her get angry with you when you remind her about the dishes. Then we can work on your behavior from there.

Repeated Failure

C: Since you've been having some trouble initiating conversations with people you don't know, Carl, maybe we ought to try something else. You were very good at asking other clients here for information about themselves, so why don't you try that again this week? Your assignment will be to ask five different clients for some sort of information about themselves, like how they spent their weekend. We can practice that today and later we'll practice initiating conversations with strangers again.

Finally the counselor reminds the client of his real-life assignment. See Figure 7, page 108. Just as prompts are effective within the Training Session, they are also helpful for reminding the client to actually carry out his assignment. Figure 8 shows a cue card used at the Oxnard Mental Health Center to remind clients to follow through with their assignments. The assignment is written on the card and given to the clients after they have completed their behavioral rehearsals and have agreed on their assignment. The card is 3 x 5 inches, the size of a small index card, and can be kept in the person's wallet or purse. At the next Planning Meeting, the counselor collects the card which cues him to give positive feedback for effort and accomplishment. When all of the clients have rehearsed, have been rated, and have received their assignments, the Training Session is over. See Figure 8, page 109.

When clients are given real-life assignments to actually carry out their exercises in Personal Effectiveness, they are sometimes concerned about the reactions they will produce in others. This concern is justified. The real world and the people in it are not always predictable. People will react differently to a newly assertive person. We have found that our clients enjoy the challenges that come with change, even though some people may be baffled or get angry when the client first tries out his new skills. Most of the time, however, people will respond favorably to reasonable assertiveness. Having successful experiences, gaining approval, and obtaining compliance to requests are natural reinforcers which will strengthen Personal Effectiveness.

An example of a success experience in the real world comes from the Oxnard (California) *Press-Courier* which reported a citizen's appearance at an Oxnard City Council meeting. The newspaper related how this person raised his hand, was recognized, and stood up to speak about the enjoyable aspects of living in the city of Oxnard. The front-page article was accompanied by a congratulatory editorial which

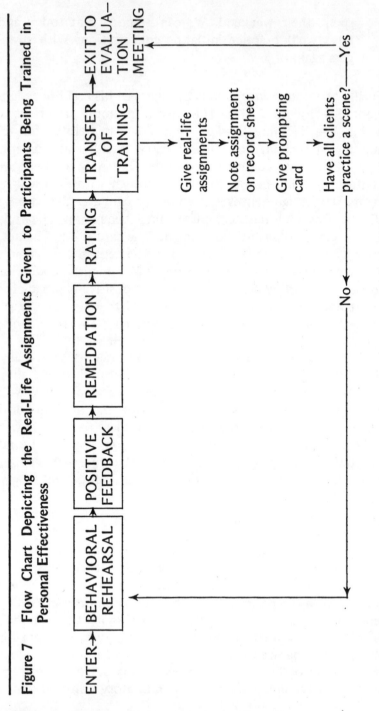

Figure 7 Flow Chart Depicting the Real-Life Assignments Given to Participants Being Trained in Personal Effectiveness

108

pointed out the rarity of such a positive event at City Council meetings. Unknown to the Council and the press was the fact that this citizen was a client completing a Personal Effectiveness assignment from the Mental Health Center. Although positive feedback may not always be provided in print, rewarding experiences usually do occur.

Figure 8   Homework Assignment Card Used to Prompt Completion of Behavioral Goals in Personal Effectiveness

---

Personal Effectiveness Training
Assignment-Report Card

Name _____

Date assignment given _____

Assignment _____

_____

_____

Date assignment due _____

Date completed _____

Counselor's initials _____

Front

Cues for Personal Effectiveness

1. Maintain EYE CONTACT

2. Use your HANDS

3. Lean TOWARD the other person

4. Pleasant FACIAL EXPRESSION

5. Speak with FIRM TONE and FLUENT pace

Back

Review Questions

Answer the following questions in the spaces provided and compare your answers with the suggested answers on pages 116-117. Discuss your answers with colleagues and reread parts of the manual if you feel it is necessary. Questions with an asterisk are open-ended and no suggested answers are given.

1. When is it advisable to have the client practice a scene with one particular person role playing, and when is it better to use a variety of people as role players?

2. When is it useful to use stock scenes?

3. Which three situations usually call for modeling?

4. Which three situations call for prompting?

5. What are some examples of prompts?

6. What is meant by a "shaping attitude"?

7. How is positive feedback related to shaping?

8. What technique or exercise can be used with quiet, withdrawn clients who speak too softly?

9. Describe the use of "Positive Statements."

10. What type of interventions might help a client who
    was not giving any response at all?

11. If a client were on the right track, and the counselor
    knew specifically what the client needed to do, what
    behavioral method would he probably use?

12. When should positive feedback be provided during a rehearsal?

13. Which three situations should prompt a decision to end a scene?

14. How should a counselor deal with a rater whose scores are markedly different from those of other group members?

*15. If you were a client, do you think you would be threatened or upset by any of the Training Session activities? Would you have a preference (either as a client or as a counselor) for any of the techniques?

*16. Do you think Personal Effectiveness would be more effective as an individual treatment or as a group treatment?

*17. Can you think of any clinical or educational situations you've recently encountered in which you could have made use of the methods discussed in this section? How about a personal situation that required more assertiveness on your part than you showed?

*18. Do you think Personal Effectiveness is similar to any other treatments with which you are familiar? How are they alike? How do they differ? Do you think one treatment would be superior for some problems?

Suggested Answers

1. It is advisable to have the client do a scene with a particular role player when he will be directing the practiced behavior in real life towards a particular person whom the role player resembles in some ways. It is better to use a variety of people when the behavior will not be directed towards any particular person in real life.

2. Stock scenes can be used in the following ways:

   1. To "warm up" a group at any point in the Training Session.

   2. To provide the counselor with an objective assessment of a client's skills in expressive behaviors prior to goal setting.

   3. To break up a session that has extended beyond the attentive limits of the group members.

3. Modeling is usually called for in the following instances:

   1. With new clients.

   2. When teaching relatively complex behaviors.

   3. When dealing with nonverbal, expressive qualities.

4. Prompting is called for in these cases:

   1. With clients who are reluctant to do or say anything or who are too inhibited to imitate modeled behavior.

   2. When dealing with simple behaviors.

   3. When concentrating on verbal behavior.

5. Some examples of prompts are given below:

   1. Hand signals

   2. Doubling

   3. Verbal prompts

6. A "shaping attitude" refers to the skill and readiness of a counselor to reward even slight improvements that are bringing the client nearer to his ultimate goals.

7. Positive feedback or social reinforcement is the primary means by which behavior is rewarded and strengthened in Personal Effec-

tiveness. The client's adaptive behavior is shaped by the strategic and contingent application of positive feedback.

8. The "standing across the room" method, called "Speak a Little Louder," can be used with quiet, withdrawn clients who speak too softly.

9. The rehearsal of positive statements can help to alter the mood of depressed clients or those with negative attitudes. The client is asked to talk for a definite period of time about something without being critical or complaining.

10. If a student is giving no response (and if a simple prompt would not be effective), modeling or doubling and then fading would be appropriate interventions.

11. If a client were on the right track and the counselor knew specifically what the client needed to do, prompting and shaping would be appropriate interventions.

12. Positive feedback should be used in the midst of a scene:

    1. When a client seems to be unsure of himself and probably needs some encouragement.

    2. When he has repeatedly attempted some behavior and finally accomplishes it satisfactorily.

    3. When the reinforcement is such that it won't cause interruption (smiling, nodding the head, "bug-in-the-ear" device).

13. Three situations that should prompt a decision to end a scene are the following:

    1. When the scene seems to be too difficult and no progress is being made.

    2. When the client is becoming increasingly anxious.

    3. When he has successfully rehearsed a scene and additional performance would be superfluous.

14. A rater giving a markedly discrepant score should be asked to explain his rating. If relevant, discussion may help to resolve the discrepancy.

Practice Exercises

The counselor can, with a colleague or fellow student, take turns playing the parts of Dick and the counselor. The person playing the counselor's role should read the dialogues aloud, improvise where indicated, and discuss each exercise before going on to the next one.

Exercise 4

C: Dick, you wanted to work on your problem with your friend, Bob, who doesn't know when to go home when he visits you, and you end up with him staying for dinner. Is there anyone you'd like to work with?

Dick: Yes, Angela.

Improvise. . . .

Dick: I'd also like to try asking him to return the money he owes me, too.

Improvise . . . .

Exercise 5

C: Go ahead and try the scene now with Harold, Dick.

Dick: I'm not sure how to sit, or what to do with my hands.

Improvise . . . .

Dick: It's getting sort of late, don't you think so?

Harold: Oh, I don't know. I think I'll sit around here for a little while longer.

Dick: I think that . . . (pause) . . . .

Improvise . . . .

Harold: What are you having for dinner?

Dick: (Smiling sheepishly) What are you getting at?

Improvise . . . .

Harold: I'm getting sort of hungry.

Dick: (Softly) Bob, I really think that it's time for you to run along.

Improvise . . . .

Dick: I'm annoyed that you're always mooching off me and I am especially angry because you haven't paid back the money I gave you three months ago.

Improvise . . . .

Exercise 6

C: Dick, you had a little trouble with your assignment last week. You were supposed to tell your friend, Bob, to leave before you ate dinner last Saturday, but he ended up staying anyway. What would you like to work on this week?

Dick: I think I'd like to try not letting him even come in the house when he comes over on Saturday.

Improvise . . . .

Exercise 7

Imagine that Dick has just rehearsed a scene and has received ratings of "4" in everything but eye contact where he received a "2." Take turns role playing the counselor reacting to the ratings and asking raters to document the reasons for their ratings.

Exercise 8

Role play Dick and a counselor working on positive statements.

Exercise 9

To gain greater empathy with clients and students who are going through training in Personal Effectiveness, each individual learning the counselor's role should pick one of the following real-life assignments and carry it out. The results of trying these homework assignments should be discussed in a group.

1. Go to a coffee shop or cafe, sit down and request a glass of water without ordering any food.

2. Drive into a service station and ask the attendant to check your oil and water and wash the windshield without purchasing any gasoline.

3. Go into an expensive clothing store or boutique and tell the salesperson you don't wish to purchase anything, but you would like to try on one of the expensive garments.

4. Go into an auto dealer's showroom, tell the salesperson that while you aren't interested in buying a car now, you would like to have a test drive.

Chapter 4

The Evaluation Meeting

After the Training Session, the counselors or co-leaders should meet for about ten minutes to evaluate and critique the activities and outcome of the training. Clients or group members should be encouraged to attend this evaluation since it provides them with additional feedback as well as an opportunity to make inputs into the leader's and counselor's behavior. The evaluation covers the following:

1. The *clients'* performances and reports of homework assignments.

2. *Staff* leadership performance and training skills.

The meeting allows for an analysis of Personal Effectiveness activities from a number of different perspectives. Counselors offer their appraisal of their own clients and other counselor's clients and reciprocally get feedback on their own performances. In this way each client and counselor can benefit from the ideas of the entire staff. Mutual feedback is especially crucial when two or more small groups are training separately at the same time in a treatment program. Openness, self-criticism, and improvement in staff performance is facilitated by the liberal use of positive feedback as well as criticism. Criticism should always be constructive and behavioral alternatives should be offered. The professional consultant is important in the Evaluation Meeting and serves an essential function in building morale and stimulating learning for the clinical staff, many of whom may be paraprofessionals, students or volunteers. The following issues are discussed during the post-training Evaluation Meeting.

Evaluating the Client's Performance

Each client's performance should be discussed in terms of its positive and negative aspects. Counselors should consider the client's performance for the particular day's session and also his overall progress. The purpose of these discussions is to evaluate the course of training with each client and to consider alternative training methods and goals. It is necessary to ask the following questions:

1. Is the client making progress in Personal Effectiveness sessions?

2. Are present training methods effectively helping the client?

3. Are the client's goals appropriate or are they too easy or too difficult?

Is the Client Making Progress?

When considering the client's progress in Personal Effectiveness sessions, the following areas should be considered and discussed:

1. *Spontaneous participation.* Is the client voluntarily and frequently taking part in scenes or must he be prodded? To maximally benefit from Personal Effectiveness, the client should "get into" the session as spontaneously as possible. If he is extremely reluctant to join in, it may be because he is disinterested in the chosen goals, or possibly afraid. Counselors should consider ways to involve students who are not actively participating, e.g., by using different techniques, by having the student work with a particular counselor or other student who may be able to arouse interest, or by selecting a more relevant and emotionally laden goal.

2. *Rehearsals.* Is the client successfully rehearsing scenes? Are deficiencies caused by a lack of understanding, a lack of ability, inhibition, or are they possibly the result of an intentional negative attitude? A "shaping atti-

tude" will often help overcome these problems. It may be necessary to have the client try easier scenes and proceed at a slower pace. For a persistently negative attitude, it may be necessary to counsel him individually, encourage expression of feelings, or ignore the negative attitude while prompting and modeling constructive, alternative behavior. Another strategy is to use paradoxical intention by giving the negative client instructions not to engage in behavioral rehearsal.

3. *Positive feedback.* Counselors should discuss the way in which their clients give feedback to each other. Is the client giving ratings? Are they too high? Are they too low? Is there a purposeful negative attitude and sabotaging behind grossly inaccurate ratings, or are they the result of not paying attention? Negative ratings may call for systematic ignoring or individual counseling whereas those resulting from inattentiveness may be rectified by asking the client to verbally document his ratings more often during the Training Session.

4. *Generalization to natural settings.* Are the client's achievements in Personal Effectiveness sessions matched by successes in real life? If not, is it because the real-life situation does not correspond to scenes practiced in Personal Effectiveness, because more practice in the sessions is needed, or because easier assignments are necessary? Questioning the client and other staff members on these possibilities could help progress.

Below is an example of counselors discussing a client who seems to be progressing in Personal Effectiveness, but who is not reporting real-life improvement.

C_1: I don't know what Tim's problem is. He is doing fine in the Training Sessions, but he seems to be having trouble with his assignments.

C_2: Do you think he's absorbing the skills he's learning in Personal Effectiveness?

C_1: Well, he's attentive and serious during the sessions.

C_3: You're right. I don't think it's as much a matter of his not learning as it is a matter of his not performing outside.

C_1: Do you think easier assignments would help?

C_3: Yes. Give him a chance to see himself being effective in real life.

C_2: Then you can gradually increase the difficulty of the assignments.

C_1: Yes, I'll try that.

Are the Training Methods Helping the Client?

If a client is not making progress, the counselors may want to evaluate the effectiveness of their techniques. They may try to improve the client's progress by using other techniques or "Tricks for Treatment" (see p. 84). In some cases they may modify the treatment goals at the same time that they implement different methods. For instance, if a client were making no progress when modeling had been used to improve gestures, eye contact and voice loudness, the counselors might make progress by establishing a more modest goal, such as having him practice speaking more loudly by the "a little louder" method.

When progress is being made, counselors should point out which methods seem to be particularly effective with the client. During the Evaluation Meeting counselors should give credit to each other when their own training skills lead to clear improvement in their clients' behavior. Therefore, when evaluating progress, the counselors should consider their leadership behavior and the effects of that behavior on the client.

Are the Goals Appropriate?

If the client is not reporting successful completion of homework assignments, or if progress is not being made in the Personal Effectiveness sessions, the counselor may have to reassess his goals. This is especially true with new students whose assets and limitations are just beginning to become familiar to the counselor. He may have to break down target behaviors into simpler components or even choose different goals altogether.

In some cases the client may require additional extrinsic motivation to follow through on assignments. Contingencies of reinforcement or rewards can be used to encourage the client to carry out assignments. For example, the client can earn points or credits, cigarettes, lunch out with a staff member, or a free movie when one or more assignments are completed in real life. Below is an example of a reward condition being established for a client who has not been attempting to carry out real-life assignments.

C: Fred, would you like to try the same assignment again next week?

Fred: OK.

C: I'll tell you what, Fred. If you carry out your assignment to initiate three conversations with your roommates, you can go with me on that bicycle tour next Saturday.

Fred: Great!

C: If you also get one of your roommates to lend you the lecture notes you missed, we'll reduce your clinic fee by half for this month.

For clients who have completed assignments regularly, new goals should be discussed and pinpointed. The counselors assume "shaping attitudes" as they consider the ultimate training goals for their group members. Successive session-by-session goals should approach the ultimate goal by small steps. The counselor asks himself where the client should be going, how he should be getting there, and how fast he should be going. See Figure 9, page 126.

Evaluating Outcome of Personal Effectiveness
While discussions among staff members after the Training Session are helpful to refine and polish the clinical *process* in

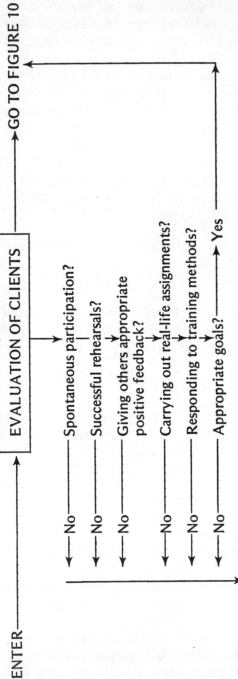

Figure 9   Flow Chart Depicting the Dimensions Used to Evaluate the Progress Made by Clients

126

Personal Effectiveness, systematic methods are needed for assessing *outcome* that are both clinically meaningful and scientifically objective and reliable. Three sources of evaluation are available and convenient for monitoring the progress of clients as they learn Personal Effectiveness: self-report of the clients themselves; observations of the client's behavior by others; and permanent products as the end results of Personal Effectiveness. These are all valid means for evaluating the progress of individual clients or of the entire treatment itself.

1. *Self-report.* The easiest and least expensive way to evaluate outcome is to simply ask the client about his progress. Clients can keep track of progress by making detailed descriptions of their experiences in carrying out real-life assignments. The more detailed the descriptions are, the more the counselor can feel confident that the report is valid. Descriptions can be made immediately after the assignment is completed in the form of a diary or log; alternatively, but less reliably, the report can be made retrospectively at the time of the next Personal Effectiveness session (see Chapter 2: The Planning Meeting). Self-reports of progress can be made using an Inventory of Assertiveness (Rathus, 1973; Wolpe and Lazarus, 1966) or by means of a yes/no response to a check on attainment of the specific goal pinpointed as the homework assignment in real life. In the Appendix (p. 141) are sample inventories as well as several sample forms which have been used by counselors and therapists to record therapeutic progress in Personal Effectiveness. Clients can report on their feelings during their acts of assertion, even estimating the degree of discomfort by referring to an arbitrary scale of "subjective units of discomfort" that might range from 0-100 or 0-10. Clients can simply report about whether or not they completed the assignment which was given to them; e.g., did they or did they not actualize the behavior which was rehearsed during the Training Session? Similarly, the frequency with which other people violate the rights of a client can be reported

as a reflection of progress in learning Personal Effectiveness. For example, if a student is being coached to stand up to a roommate who plays his stereo records too loud, the frequency of excessively loud blaring of the stereo during each week can reflect the presence or lack of response to counseling. Since the purpose of training in Personal Effectiveness is to obtain desired consequences and reactions from others, the frequency of occurrence of such end results can be a meaningful indicator of progress.

2. *Observation of behavior.* The behavior of the client can be rated directly by an observer and reported to the counselor. Observers can be family members, friends, or staff members themselves. The use of staff members as observers is particularly convenient and meaningful when the client is participating in a day treatment or residential treatment setting and the behavioral assignments can be given for completion in the facility itself. Observers can be taught to make reliable ratings of the nonverbal and verbal components of assertiveness, either directly or indirectly from video tapes and audio tapes. Much of the research done on assertion training, annotated in the Bibliography (p. 151), has used this approach to measure the outcome of therapy. The sample record forms in the Appendix have places for observers to rate the client on nonverbal dimensions, such as eye contact, voice volume, gestures, and posture. Observers can also report whether or not a participant has actually performed the assigned task or how well he has resisted pressures from others that would violate his rights.

3. *Permanent products.* Many times successful completion of homework assignments in Personal Effectiveness produces some type of tangible, permanent product. A wife given an assignment to ask her husband to take her out for a social evening can bring ticket stubs from the theater or a menu from a restaurant to the next treatment session, thereby demonstrating success to the

counselor. A young man who practices taking job interviews in Personal Effectiveness can bring to the next session a completed job application or, even better, a stub from a salary check. Permanent products of assertive acts reflect the favorable reactions to the personally effective client from his social environment.

Monitoring progress in a systematic and rigorous way not only benefits the client, but it also enables the counselor to accumulate valid feedback on the relative success of training methods with a variety of problems and populations. In this way, the entire field of counseling and therapy, and the professionals attempting to advance it, can move ahead with developing and evaluating new methods. An empirical attitude with a tight bond and commitment to measurement of results will minimize the magical and sometimes superstitious attachment to fads and methods, and will provide therapists with data to improve and change their clinical efforts.

Evaluating Staff Performance

During the Evaluation Meeting the counselors should discuss the following points for self-improvement:

1. Using techniques.

2. Setting goals.

3. Using clients and staff.

Using Techniques

Counselors should point out to each other techniques that seemed to be particularly effective. For example, one counselor might say to another, "I thought it really helped when you had Tony stand across the room to talk about himself, Bob. It was the first time I could hear everything he was saying." In addition, techniques which did not seem to be effective should be noted and other methods suggested as substitutes. When assisting colleagues with feedback, a counselor should consider the situational guidelines for using a particular technique which were outlined in Chapter 3, p. 97. In some cases the appraisal of the situation will depend upon the combined observations of a number of counselors, each offering his own perspective.

The counselors in the following discussion assist each other in determining a client's problems and how this determination facilitates the planning of a treatment strategy.

C_1: I don't feel like I'm getting anywhere with Carrie.

C_2: I think you're right. She does OK in here, but she never carries out her assignments.

C_1: She seems to have gotten down the knack of initiating conversations, but she just won't try it outside of the Personal Effectiveness sessions.

C_3: I disagree about her progress in training. She can initiate conversations, but have you ever noticed that it's always about the same thing? She doesn't talk about anything but sewing.

C_1: Now that you mention it, you're right.

C_4: She usually rehearses with women, too, so she can plan on having at least some success with that topic.

C_2: It would probably be a good idea to have her rehearse with men as well as women.

C_1: Right, and also to have her talk about other things besides sewing.

C_3: Why don't you have her initiate conversations with men and women here at the Center as an assignment?

C_1: Good idea. I think I'll also make seconds for dessert at lunch contingent upon her starting at least three conversations with men and three with women during the next two days.

C_4: Don't you think it would be better practice for her to talk to strangers rather than to people here?

C_1: I think that would be more useful later on, but for now

I'd just like to get her going. Also, using people here allows us to validate her reports.

Other areas of discussion may include variations in the use of methods, strategies for intervention, reinforcing reports of generalization to real-life situations, and new techniques.

Setting Goals
Counselors should discuss the adequacy of the goals that have been set for clients.

1. Are they realistic?
   Are they achievable?
   Are they functional (useful in the real world)?

2. Are successive small or weekly goals bringing the client to an ultimate goal at an appropriate pace?

3. Is the attainment of goals in training matched by real-life achievements?

Using Clients and Staff
The following questions should be considered when appraising the staff's use of clients and other counselors to facilitate the activities of the Training Session:

1. Is each client participating?

2. Are counselors encouraging "wallflower" clients to get involved? Can some clients be used to get other clients involved?

3. Do staff members make use of each other's unique talents?

4. Do some clients or staff members work particularly well with a specific client?

5. Are counselors eliciting positive feedback from clients?

Other topics for discussion may center around the *mechanics of the Personal Effectiveness session.* Were the practice scenes too long? How were disruptive behaviors or evasive tactics handled? Are staff members working toward keeping scenes short with contingent, positive acknowledgment?

Post-session discussions may result in suggestions for the improvement of future Personal Effectiveness meetings. Counselors should highlight particularly effective techniques and maneuvers such as video tape feedback, remote control prompting, and arranging special reward conditions. Staff members are encouraged to comment on their own performance at this session. Critical self-evaluation is particularly helpful when training new staff, students, or visitors in the techniques required to lead a successful Personal Effectiveness group. Critical feedback from the clients or participants is also useful.

Each Evaluation Meeting need not cover in detail all of the points mentioned in this section, but the staff should evaluate the sessions with these topics in mind. Holding a meeting specifically for this kind of feedback is an excellent way to reinforce staff members' progress in leading Personal Effectiveness groups (see Figure 10).

Figure 10 Flow Chart Depicting the Procedures Used in the Evaluation Meeting to Discuss and Critique Staff Performance

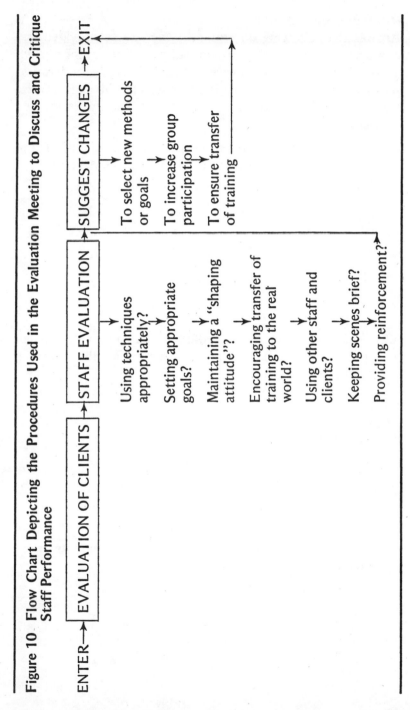

ENTER → EVALUATION OF CLIENTS → STAFF EVALUATION → SUGGEST CHANGES → EXIT

STAFF EVALUATION:
- Using techniques appropriately?
- Setting appropriate goals?
- Maintaining a "shaping attitude"?
- Encouraging transfer of training to the real world?
- Using other staff and clients?
- Keeping scenes brief?
- Providing reinforcement?

SUGGEST CHANGES:
- To select new methods or goals
- To increase group participation
- To ensure transfer of training

Review Questions

Answer the following questions in the spaces provided and compare your answers with the suggested answers on pages 138-139. Discuss your answers with colleagues and reread relevant parts of the manual if you have any difficulty. Questions with an asterisk are open-ended and no suggested answers are given.

1. Which two major areas of performance during the Training Session are critiqued in the Evaluation Meeting?

2. Which three questions should be asked about the participation of each client or student in the Personal Effectiveness group?

3. What can be done to get clients or students more involved in Personal Effectiveness?

4. What are some possible courses of action if the client's goals do not seem to be appropriate?

5. What are the three major areas of discussion in the evaluation of staff performance?

6. When considering a client's goals, what are three dimensions that the staff should consider?

7. When evaluating the staff's use of clients and each other, what are some important considerations?

*8. Do you feel that the Evaluation Meeting will contribute to the success of subsequent Personal Effectiveness sessions?

*9. Can you foresee any instances in which the Evaluation Meeting may be counterproductive? Do you think that its success depends upon harmonious staff relationships?

*10. How would you feel if you encountered a lot of criticism with regard to your handling of a client? How would you respond to it?

*11. Do you think it is important to be critical as well as laudatory during the Evaluation Meeting, or should the emphasis be on positive feedback only?

Suggested Answers

1. The two major areas critiqued in the Evaluation Meeting are listed below:

   1. The client's performance and homework assignment reports.
   2. The leadership performance and training skills of the staff.

2. Below are the three questions that should be asked about each client:

   1. Is the client making progress in Personal Effectiveness sessions?
   2. Are present training methods effectively helping the client?
   3. Are the client's goals appropriate?

3. To involve clients more in Personal Effectiveness, counselors should consider using different techniques, more relevant goals, or having the client work with a particular counselor or fellow client who may be able to arouse interest.

4. If the client's goals appear too difficult, it may be necessary to break down target behaviors into simpler components or even to redefine target behaviors. Another possibility is to establish reinforcement contingencies for completed assignments.

5. The major areas of discussion in the evaluation of staff performance are the following:
   1. The use of behavioral techniques.
   2. Setting goals.
   3. The use of clients and staff in the training process.

6. When considering client's goals, the staff should be asking themselves these questions:
   1. Are the goals realistic, achievable, and functional?
   2. Are successive goals bringing the client closer to an ultimate goal at an appropriate pace?
   3. Is the attainment of goals in training sessions matched by real-life achievements?

7. Important considerations for evaluating the staff's use of clients and each other are the following:

   1. Is each client participating?
   2. Are counselors encouraging wallflower clients to get involved? Can some clients be used to get other clients involved?

3. Do staff members make use of each other's unique talents?
4. Would some clients or staff work particularly well with a specific client?
5. Are counselors eliciting positive feedback from clients?

Practice Exercise

With your colleagues or fellow students, work as a group and role play counselors evaluating a Training Session of Personal Effectiveness. Refer to clients you have previously practiced with, or describe a client to the group and relate his activities during the Training Session. The advantage of making up a new hypothetical client is that the entire group will then be familiar with him.

Appendix
Recording Forms for Evaluating Personal Effectiveness

Sample forms for recording therapeutic progress in Personal Effectiveness are provided here as guidelines for therapists and counselors, who are encouraged to monitor their clients' real-life performance and accomplishment during training. Without systematic recordkeeping, the techniques described in this manual can lose their effectiveness and remain only a "fad." There are no "absolutes" in choosing criteria for assessing the outcome of training in Personal Effectiveness. However, the form for evaluating the outcome of Personal Effectiveness training (page 143) indicates some of the dimensions that are relevant.

The sample forms were all used to evaluate clinical programs at the Oxnard Mental Health Center and Camarillo State Hospital. They combine self-reporting and staff observation as the sources of information for evaluating the impact of training in Personal Effectiveness. Observers subjectively rate the quality of the client's performance during the behavioral rehearsal; the clients and staff both assess whether or not the assigned behavioral goal was carried out in the natural setting.

Possible Strategies for Evaluating the Outcome of Training in Personal Effectiveness

Type of Data	Source of Evaluation		
	Self-report	Observer	Permanent Products
Detailed narrative descriptions: logs, diaries, verbal reports			
Feelings, subjective mood			
Actual enactment of behavior rehearsed in Training Session			
Frequency of violations against self-rights			
Check list of behaviors performed			
Ratings of verbal and nonverbal behaviors			
Favorable reactions or desired end results to behavior from environment			

Personal Effectiveness Record Sheet

Name _____ Date _____

Date	Behavioral Practice							Behavioral Assignment	Date Assignment Completed	Date of Spontaneous Occurrence
	Eye Contact	Use of Hands	Facial Expressions	Posture	Voice Loudness	Speech Fluency	Speech Content			

Behavioral Goals

1.

2.

3.

4.

5.

6.

Personal Effectiveness Training Record

Name_____ Date _____

Goal: _____
_____
_____
_____

Rating:
1—Work needed
2—Improved
3—Good

Behavior Components:

Body Language	Date					Trials					
Eye Contact											
Gestures—Descriptive											
—Emphatic											
Posture											
Facial Expression											

Verbalization

Volume											
Tone											
Frequency											
Fluency											
Modulation											

Content

Appropriate to Situation											
Attentive											
Reinforcing to Others											
Stressing Positives											

Assertiveness Inventory

Name_____ Date_____

Yes or No

_____ 1. When a person is blatantly unfair, do you usually say something about it to him?

_____ 2. Are you always very careful to avoid all trouble with other people?

_____ 3. Do you often avoid social contacts for fear of doing or saying the wrong thing?

_____ 4. If a friend betrays your confidence, do you tell him how you really feel?

_____ 5. If you had a roommate, would you insist that he do his fair share of the cleaning?

_____ 6. When a clerk in a store waits on someone who has come in after you, do you call his attention to the matter?

_____ 7. Are there very few people with whom you can be relaxed and have a good time?

_____ 8. Would you be hesitant about asking a good friend to lend you a few dollars?

_____ 9. If someone who has borrowed $5 from you seems to have forgotten about it, would you remind this person?

_____10. If a person keeps on teasing you, do you have difficulty expressing your annoyance or displeasure?

_____11. Would you remain standing at the rear of a crowded auditorium rather than looking for a seat up front?

_____12. If someone keeps kicking the back of your chair in a movie, would you ask him to stop?

_____13. If a friend keeps calling you very late each evening, would you ask him not to call after a certain time?

_____14. If someone starts talking to someone else right in the middle of your conversation, do you express your irritation?

_____15. In a plush restaurant, if you order a medium steak and find it too raw, would you ask the waiter to have it recooked?

_____16. If the landlord of your apartment fails to make certain necessary repairs after promising to do so, would you insist upon it?

_____17. Would you return a faulty garment you purchased a few days ago?

_____18. If someone you respect expresses opinions with which you strongly disagree, would you venture to state your own point of view?

_____19. Are you usually able to say "no" if people make unreasonable requests?

_____20. Do you think that people should stand up for their rights?

_____21. Do you protest verbally when someone pushes in front of you in a line?

_____22. Are you inclined to be overly apologetic?

_____23. A friend unjustifiably criticizes you. Do you express your reaction openly?

_____24. Are you able to contradict a domineering person?

_____25. You hear that another person is spreading false rumors about you. Would you go to him directly to correct the situation?

_____26. Do you usually keep your opinions to yourself?

_____27. Are you able to openly express love and affection?

_____28. Do you tell your friends you care for them?

_____29. Do you take the initiative to cut telephone calls short when you are busy?

_____30. If after leaving a shop you notice that you have been given short change, do you go back and point out the error?

Assertiveness Schedule

Directions: Indicate how characteristic or descriptive each of the following statements is of you by using the code given below:

+3 very characteristic of me, extremely descriptive

+2 rather characteristic of me, quite descriptive

+1 somewhat characteristic of me, slightly descriptive

-1 somewhat uncharacteristic of me, slightly nondescriptive

-2 rather uncharacteristic of me, quite nondescriptive

-3 very uncharacteristic of me, extremely nondescriptive

Total score obtained by adding numerical responses to each item, after changing the signs of reversed items, which are indicated by an asterisk (*).

_____ 1. Most people seem to be more aggressive and assertive than I am.*

_____ 2. I have hesitated to make or accept dates because of "shyness."*

_____ 3. When the food served at a restaurant is not done to my satisfaction, I complain about it to the waiter or waitress.

_____ 4. I am careful to avoid hurting other people's feelings, even when I feel that I have been injured.*

_____ 5. If a salesman has gone to considerable trouble to show me merchandise which is not quite suitable, I have a difficult time saying "No."*

_____ 6. When I am asked to do something, I insist upon knowing why.

_____ 7. There are times when I look for a good, vigorous argument.

_____ 8. I strive to get ahead as well as most people in my position.

_____ 9. To be honest, people often take advantage of me.*

_____10. I enjoy starting conversations with new acquaintances and strangers.

_____11. I often don't know what to say to attractive people of the opposite sex.*

_____12. I hesitate to make phone calls to business establishments and institutions.*

_____ 13. I would rather apply for a job or for admission to a college by writing letters than by going through with personal interviews.*

_____ 14. I find it embarrassing to return merchandise.*

_____ 15. If a close and respected relative were annoying me, I would hide my feelings rather than express my annoyance.*

_____ 16. I have avoided asking questions for fear of sounding stupid.*

_____ 17. During an argument I am sometimes afraid that I will get so upset that I will shake all over.*

_____ 18. If a famed and respected lecturer makes a statement which I think is incorrect, I will have the audience hear my point of view as well.

_____ 19. I avoid arguing over prices with clerks and salesmen.*

_____ 20. When I have done something important or worthwhile, I manage to let others know about it.

_____ 21. I am open and frank about my feelings.

_____ 22. If someone has been spreading false and bad stories about me, I see him as soon as possible to "have a talk" about it.

_____ 23. I often have a hard time saying "No."*

_____ 24. I tend to bottle up my emotions rather than make a scene.*

_____ 25. I complain about poor service in a restaurant and elsewhere.

_____ 26. When I am given a compliment, I sometimes just don't know what to say.*

_____ 27. If a couple near me in a theatre or at a lecture were conversing rather loudly, I would ask them to be quiet or to take their conversation elsewhere.

_____ 28. Anyone attempting to push ahead of me in line is in for a good battle.

_____ 29. I am quick to express an opinion.

_____ 30. There are times when I just can't say anything.*

Reprinted with permission from Rathus, S. A. A 30-Item Schedule for Assessing Assertive Behavior. *Behavior Therapy*, 1973, *4*, 398-406.

Annotated Bibliography

Alberti, R. E., & Emmons, M. L. *Your perfect right.* San Luis Obispo, CA.: Impact Press, 1974.

This is a small manual describing the theory and practice of Assertion Training with neurotic or other mildly deficient individuals. The authors work in a university counseling center and their experience derives from training shy and withdrawn students. Clearly and simply written with a minimum of jargon, it is a very popular and useful introduction. No research evidence is presented. The book is suitable for reading by lay people as well as by professionals in the helping fields. Part I is a rationale and description of assertiveness in everyday life and is written for the layman. Part II contains material on counseling methods and pitfalls and is aimed at the clinician.

Bandura, A. *Principles of behavior modification.* New York: Holt, Rinehart and Winston, 1969.

Chapter 3 reviews the role of modeling in the treatment of behavioral disorders. Through modeling processes new modes of behavior are acquired and existing response patterns are extensively modified. Subjects learn by observation of other people's behavior and through reinforcing consequences. A multi-process theory of observational learning is formulated by the author. Modeling procedures are described for developing conceptual and interpersonal modes of behavior, and for the vicarious extinction of maladaptive emotional behavior. This book is one of the most thorough expositions of behavior therapy, its underlying principles, and its derivation from laboratory-based experimental psychology. Bandura, one of the principal developers of social learning theory, emphasizes the importance of cognitive and covert mental processes as intervening variables in learning new behavior. His own research in modeling and imitation provides him with manifold examples of the central importance of learning through observation in human behavior.

Bennett, P. S., & Maley, R. G. Modification of interactive behaviors in chronic mental patients. *Journal of Applied Behavior Analysis,* 1973, *6,* 609-620.

Four patients attended ten 30-minute treatment sessions where they received instructions to perform in four distinct phases of interpersonal behavior: talking to another person; attending and talking to another person, asking and answering questions in a dyad; and working cooperatively in a dyad to solve problems. Contingent reinforcement was given for interacting according to instructions. The results indicated a strong effect on performance of the target behaviors, as well as generalization to other areas of social behavior away from the treatment setting.

Blanchard, E. B., & Hersen, M. Behavioral treatment of hysterical neurosis: Symptom substitution and symptom return reconsidered. Submitted to *Archives of General Psychiatry,* 1974.

This article presents the psychoanalytic and behavioral positions on symptom substitution and symptom return. Four cases of hysterical, conversion neurosis treated with behavioral techniques are presented to illustrate these phenomena. A three component treatment program is recommended utilizing extinction procedures for symptom manifestation, instructions to the patients' social environment, and teaching the patient new social skills.

Bloomfield, H. Assertive Training in an outpatient group of chronic schizophrenics: A preliminary report. *Behavior Therapy,* 1973, *4,* 277-281.

Chronic schizophrenics tend to be excessively compliant, submissive, and socially inhibited. Assertive Training for outpatients was successful in decreasing their social anxiety, and increasing their range of interpersonal skills. A case example is given to illustrate the step-by-step application of Assertive Training.

Davis, J. R. Treating inappropriate nonverbal behaviors by immediate video and therapist feedback. Unpublished manuscript. Available from the author at Camarillo-Neuropsychiatric Institute Research Center, Box A, Camarillo, CA.

A 28-year-old man with interpersonally debilitating movements of his face, hands, arms, torso, and legs received immediate visual and auditory feedback for five 15-minute sessions, three times daily. Inappropriate bodily movements decreased by 50-90 percent, but the improvements did not generalize to other settings.

Eckman, T. A. The educational workshop model as a treatment alternative in a partial hospitalization program. Unpublished manuscript. Available from the author at the Oxnard, California Community Mental Health Center.

This article describes the assessment of a day treatment program and subsequent developments of a highly structured program based on community survival skills, presented in educational workshop format. Content of workshop, implementation considerations, and evaluation procedures are described.

Edwards, N. B. Case conference: Assertive Training in a case of homosexual pedophilia. *Journal of Behavior Therapy and Experimental Psychiatry*, 1972, *3*, 55-63.

A case of homosexual pedophilia of 10 years' duration was seen at a time when the patient's family was disintegrating in consequence of his deviation. At his first session he was trained in thought-stopping in order to diminish his preoccupation with pedophilic fantasies and the anxiety they produced. He then went overseas for a month, during which time the thought-stopping proved notably effective. Upon his return, he was schooled in assertive behavior which led, apparently, to an elimination of the interpersonal anxieties which had interfered with normal heterosexual functioning and led to the pedophilia. The patient attained normal social and sexual function in the course of 13 interviews.

Eisler, R. M. Assertive Training in the work situation. In J. D. Krumboltz, & Carl E. Thoresen (Eds.), *Behavioral counseling methods.* New York: Holt, Rinehart and Winston, in press.

The case of a 39-year-old unassertive male is presented, who was video taped (pre and post) while responding to six simulated scenes. The scenes were relevant to his problem situation, and required assertive responses. Training utilized behavioral rehearsal, therapist modeling and feedback, and included five sessions with ten rehearsals per scene. In general, results were positive and assertive behaviors had generalized to real-life situations, with maintenance reported at three- and seven-month follow-ups.

Eisler, R. M., & Hersen, M. Behavioral techniques in family-oriented crisis intervention. *Archives of General Psychiatry*, 1973, *28*, 111-116.

Behavioral techniques in short-term family-oriented crisis intervention is examined in this article. These methods include feedback, modeling, behavioral rehearsal, instructions, and behavioral contracts. Three cases are presented to illustrate the therapeutic flexibility of these techniques with crisis-prone families, and the preventive advantage of learning problem-solving skills that can be implemented daily.

Eisler, R. M., Hersen, M., & Agras, W. S. Effects of video tape and instructional feedback on nonverbal marital interaction: An analog study. *Behavior Therapy*, 1973, *4*, 551-558.

A series of analog studies was conducted to examine the separate and combined effects of video tape feedback and focused instructions. Video tape feedback in the absence of instructions effected a slight increase in nonverbal interactions (looking and smiling) of 12 married couples, while focused instructions led to marked changes in looking. Combining video tape feedback and focused instructions was not significantly more effective than instructions alone on looking, but did produce an increase in smiling.

Eisler, R. M., Hersen, M., & Agras, W. S. Video tape: A method for the controlled observation of nonverbal interpersonal behavior. *Behavior Therapy*, 1973, *4*, 420-425.

The authors assess the reliability and practical utility of video tape in observing the looking and smiling behaviors of six married couples as compared with "live" observations of the same dyadic behavior. They also explore the feasibility and advantages of rating similar nonverbal interactive behaviors (mutual looking and smiling) from video tape replays. The results indicate that reliability of video observations is as high as for the observations of the same "live" behavior, and that video tape facilitates relatively precise definitions of behaviors.

154

Eisler, R. M., Hersen, M., & Miller, P. M. Effects of modeling on components of assertive behavior. *Journal of Behavior Therapy and Experimental Psychiatry*, 1973, *4*, 1-6.

Thirty male hospitalized psychiatric patients who observed a video taped male model were compared with similar patients who merely practiced their responses, and with untreated controls on eight verbal and nonverbal components of assertiveness measured in a variety of stimulus situations. The simulated real-life situations were video taped (pre and post), and a female assistant played the standardized counter roles. The modeling group improved significantly on five of the eight components of assertiveness, whereas no difference was found for the practice-control and test-retest groups.

Eisler, R. M., Hersen, M., & Miller, P. M. Shaping components of assertive behavior with instructions and feedback. *American Journal of Psychiatry*, 1974, *131*, 1344-1347.

The application of instructions and immediate feedback via a miniature radio receiver placed in the patient's ear is described. Interactions for the two subjects were video taped and the training consisted of rehearsing standard assertive situations. Results indicated rapid acquisition of component assertive behaviors and generalization to untreated rehearsals of the patients' real-life problems.

Eisler, R. M., Hersen, M., Miller, P. M., & Blanchard, E. B. Situational determinants of assertive behaviors. *Journal of Consulting and Clinical Psychology*, 1975, *43*, 330-340.

Thirty-two assertive situations that varied in social-interpersonal context were administered to 60 hospitalized psychiatric patients via role playing. Half of the role played situations required the expression of negative (hostile) assertiveness, and the other half required positive (commendatory) assertive expression. Situational context was varied by having the subjects respond to male and female interpersonal partners who were either familiar or unfamiliar to the patients. Responses were video taped and rated on five measures of speech content and seven measures of nonverbal behavior. Additionally, groups of high- and low-assertive patients were identified from the total sample using a behavioral measure of global assertiveness and a self-report instrument. Results indicated that interpersonal behavior in assertive situations varied as a function of social context. Further, high- and low-assertive subjects were differentiated on the basis of 9 of the 12 measures of interpersonal behavior. Support for a stimulus specific theory of assertive behaviors and implications for Assertive Training are discussed.

Eisler, R. M., Miller, P. M., & Hersen, M. Components of assertive behavior. *Journal of Clinical Psychology*, 1973, *29*, 295-299.

Thirty male psychiatric patients were video taped performing fourteen standard, interpersonal situations requiring assertive responses to a female role model's prompts. The tapes were rated on nine behavioral components of assertiveness. Subjects were dichotomized into high and low assertive groups; the former tended to respond to interpersonal problems quickly, in a strongly audible voice with marked intonation, and did not automatically accede to the demands of others. Duration of looking, speech fluency and smiling did not appear to be related to judgments of assertiveness. The two groups differed significantly on the Wolpe-Lazarus Assertiveness Questionnaire.

Eisler, R. M., Miller, P. M., Hersen, M., & Alford, H. Effects of Assertive Training on marital interaction. *Archives of General Psychiatry*, 1974, *30*, 643-649.

Three couples were video taped while discussing their marital conflicts before and after the "passive" males received 45 minutes of training in assertive instruction. The training consisted of instructions, behavioral rehearsal, and feedback, but varied on structure and relevancy to each couple's marital conflicts. The husband's assertiveness improved in all three cases, with superior results from the cases where training had been more specific to the couple's interpersonal difficulties.

Fensterheim, H. Behavior therapy: Assertive Training in groups. In C. J. Sager, & H. S. Kaplan (Eds.), *Progress in group and family therapy*. New York: Brunner/Mazel, 1972.

The author discusses the use of specific behavior therapy techniques in groups, such as operant methods, relaxation training, and systematic desensitization. A "typical" Assertive Training group is described which employs the following techniques: didactic instructions, review of life situations, behavioral rehearsal, specific exercises, and assignments. A journal description of minigroup Assertive Training is included.

156

Finch, B. E., & Wallace, C. J. Successful Assertion Training with schizophrenic inpatients. Unpublished manuscript. Available from the authors at Camarillo-Neuropsychiatric Institute Research Center, Box A, Camarillo, CA.

Eight schizophrenic patients received 12 sessions of Assertion Training including behavioral rehearsal, modeling, and positive feedback during seven separate scenes. To facilitate generalization, patients were given assignments to carry out in pairs, and were encouraged to reinforce each other for completing assignments. Audiotape recordings of pre- and posttreatment interviews were rated "blindly" for four components of assertive behavior: loudness, fluency, affect, and content. Results indicated that the eight patients receiving Assertion Training did significantly better than a milieu therapy control group on all the behavioral measures and on the Wolpe-Lazarus Assertion Questionnaire. The improvement shown by the assertion group extended to both trained and untrained scenes.

Fichter, M. H., Wallace, C. J., Liberman, R. P., & Davis, J. R. Increasing social behaviors in a chronic psychotic: Experimental analysis and generalization. Unpublished manuscript. Available from the authors at Camarillo-Neuropsychiatric Institute Research Center, Box A, Camarillo, CA.

A severely withdrawn schizophrenic inpatient was allowed to escape into isolation from others contingent upon appropriate social performance in interaction sessions. Three behaviors constituted appropriate performance: (1) voice volume loud enough to be intelligible at a distance of ten feet; (2) duration of speech of at least fifteen seconds; (3) placement of elbows on the arms of a chair. A combination of multiple baseline and withdrawal designs established that the improved social behaviors were a result of the contingency. Generalization was found to occur over time, place, and responses, possibly as a result of the over 1800 training sessions conducted in the hospital.

Foy, D. W., Eisler, R. M., & Pinkston, S. Modeled assertion in a case of explosive rages. *Journal of Behavior Therapy and Experimental Psychiatry*, in press.

A 56-year-old carpenter with a history of explosive rages was given Assertive Training consisting of modeling alone, and modeling combined with instructions focused on the desirable features of the modeled behavior. Improvements from modeling alone were enhanced by the addition of instructions. The changes were maintained during six months of follow-up evaluations based on repetitions of the role played situations involved in the treatment. Self-reports indicated that improvements had generalized to the patient's natural environment.

Friedman, P. H. The effects of modeling and role playing on assertive behavior. In R. D. Rubin, H. Fensterheim, A. A. Lazarus, & C. M. Franks (Eds.), *Advances in behavior therapy.* New York: Academic Press, 1971.

One hundred college students were assigned to one of the following six conditions: (1) modeling plus role playing, (2) modeling, (3) directed role playing, (4) improvised role playing, (5) assertive script, and (6) nonassertive script. Subjects in the improvised role playing condition who rated themselves more capable of asserting themselves following role playing showed the greatest change in assertiveness.

Galassi, J. P., Galassi, M. D., & Litz, M. C. Assertive Training in groups using video feedback. *Journal of Counseling Psychology,* 1974, *21,* 390-394.

Thirty-two nonassertive male and female college students were randomly assigned to Assertive Training or control groups. The 16 students in the Assertive Training groups received eight sessions consisting of video tape modeling, behavior rehearsal, video, peer and trainer feedback plus bibliotherapy, homework assignments, trainer exhortation and peer group support. Self-report questionnaires and pre and post video taped role playing situations indicated that the students receiving Assertive Training were significantly improved over controls on the College Self-Expression Scale, the Subjective Units of Disturbance Scale, eye contact, length of scene, and assertive content.

Gittelman, M. Behavior rehearsal as a technique in child treatment. *Journal of Child Psychology and Psychiatry,* 1965, *6,* 251-255.

The clinical utility and effectiveness of behavioral rehearsal with children is illustrated by means of case anecdotes. The procedure is described and examples of results with follow-up are given.

Goldstein, A. P. *Structured learning therapy: Toward a psychotherapy for the poor.* New York: Academic Press, 1973.

Data from carefully controlled experiments done by the author and others are marshalled to document the effectiveness of the components of Structured Learning Therapy which is another term for Assertion Training or training in Personal Effectiveness. The components include modeling, role playing, social reinforcement, instructions and prompts, and efforts at generalizing the behavior change from the treatment setting to the natural environment. The author presents results from experiments using Structured Learning Therapy with lower class alcoholics, hospitalized chronic schizophrenics, and outpatient psychoneurotics. The goals of therapy were enhanced social interaction, expression of feelings to others, and independent behaviors. Verbatim scripts are provided in a 160-page Appendix to enable the readers of the book to replicate the methods used by the author. Emphasis is on practice, direct guidance by the therapists, and plentiful reinforcement. This is a landmark book, heralding a new thrust in psychiatry and clinical psychology toward structured and empirically evaluated treatment methods for patients from all social classes.

Goldstein, A. P., & Goedhart, A. The use of structured learning for empathy enhancement in paraprofessional psychotherapist training. *Journal of Community Psychology,* 1973, *1,* 168-173.

The authors report two studies where structured learning (modeling + role playing + social reinforcement) was successfully employed by professional trainers to enhance empathy among mental hospital personnel. Subjects were mainly nursing staff personnel in frequent contact with patients. Evidence was also found regarding the value of *in vivo* performance feedback as a transfer of training procedure.

Goldstein, A. P., Martens, J., Hubben, J., Van Belle, H. A., Schaaf, W., Wierema, H., & Goedhart, A. The use of modeling to increase independent behavior. *Behaviour Research and Therapy,* 1973, *11,* 31-42.

The authors describe three experiments aimed at independence via the use of modeling procedures. Two samples of neurotic outpatients and one sample of psychiatric inpatients served as subjects. Significant gains in independence emerged in all three investigations, as well as subsidiary findings regarding the possible clinical application of "modeling enhancers."

Goldstein, A. P., & Sorcher, M. Changing managerial behavior by applied learning techniques. *Training and Development Journal*, March, 1973.

Modeling, role playing, social reinforcement, and transfer of training can be specifically and successfully applied to management training. Some methods for evaluation are cited. The authors emphasize the rationale for targeting behavior change to eventually bring about attitude change.

Gutride, M. E., Goldstein, A. P., & Hunter, G. F. The use of modeling and role playing to increase social interaction among asocial clinical patients. *Journal of Consulting and Clinical Psychology*, 1973, *40*, 408-415.

Eighty-seven unassertive psychiatric patients were examined on three treatment variables: (1) structured learning therapy = modeling + role playing + social reinforcement (presence/absence), (2) psychotherapy (presence or absence) and (3) patient status (acute-chronic). Interaction effects were examined; those for structured learning therapy and psychotherapy suggested a "mutual inhibition" of treatment effectiveness.

Hersen, M., & Eisler, R. M. Social skill training. In W. E. Craighead, A. E. Kazdin, & M. J. Mahoney (Eds.), *Behavior Modification: Principles, issues and applications*. Boston: Houghton Mifflin, in press.

This chapter points out the specific deficits in social skills underlying many forms of psychopathology and conceptualizes, as a primary therapeutic task, a concerted effort to help patients develop viable social responses. The authors describe the basic technical operations used during the treatment of social-skill deficits related to depression, minimal dating, unassertiveness and schizophrenic withdrawal. The need for generalization strategies and follow-up studies is stressed.

Hersen, M., Eisler, R. M., & Miller, P. M. Development of assertive responses: Clinical, measurement, and research considerations. *Behaviour Research and Therapy*, 1973, *11*, 505-521.

In this literature review, the development of assertive responding is examined in light of clinical, measurement, and research considerations. Specific issues such as generalization of training, reinforcement of anger, and the use of the group psychotherapy approach are considered. Suggestions are made' regarding future research and clinical applications, such as more efforts at instigating positive responses, both clinically and experimentally.

Hersen, M., Eisler, R. M., & Miller, P. M. An experimental analysis of generalization in Assertive Training. *Behaviour Research and Therapy*, 1974, *12*, 295-310.

Fifty unassertive male psychiatric patients were assigned to one of the following conditions: (1) test-retest, (2) practice-control, (3) practice-control with generalization instructions, (4) modeling and instructions, (5) modeling and instructions with generalization instructions. Subjects were video taped (pre and post) while responding to ten interpersonal situations requiring assertiveness. The modeling and instruction groups effected the greatest changes on the training scenes with some generalization to similar scenes. Effects of an independent, *in vivo* test for generalization were minimal.

Hersen, M., Eisler, R. M., Miller, P. M., Johnson, M. B., & Pinkston, S. G. Effects of practice, instructions and modeling on components of assertive behavior. *Behaviour Research and Therapy*, 1973, *11*, 443-451.

Fifty male hospitalized psychiatric patients were video taped (pre and post) while they experienced one of the following conditions to assess the role of behavioral techniques in interpersonal assertiveness: (1) test-retest, (2) practice-control, (3) modeling alone, (4) focused instructions and (5) focused instructions in combination with modeling. A behavioral assertiveness test was used for evaluation of change. The results indicated that the modeling plus instructions group was superior or equal to the instructions alone or modeling alone on five of the seven components. Instructions alone or modeling alone led to the greatest improvement in the remaining two components. No difference between the remaining groups was found.

Hersen, M., Miller, P. M., & Eisler, R. M. Interactions between alcoholics and their wives: A descriptive analysis of verbal and nonverbal behavior. *Quarterly Journal of Studies on Alcohol*, 1973, *34*, 516-520.

The effects of varying the couple's conversation (alcohol versus non-alcohol verbal content) on duration of looking and speech were assessed by video taping the interactions of four middle-aged, married couples. It was found that wives looked at their alcoholic husbands more when the discussion was related to drinking than when it was not, but the husbands tended to look more at their wives when the discussion was not related to drinking.

King, L. W., Liberman, R. P., & Roberts, J. An evaluation of Personal Effectiveness Training (Assertion Training): A behavioral group therapy. Unpublished manuscript. Available from the author at Oxnard Mental Health Center, 620 S. "D" St., Oxnard, CA.

The authors describe Personal Effectiveness Training, a structured, behavioral approach to group therapy, as conducted at the Oxnard (Calif.) Community Mental Health Center. The twice-weekly groups utilized the procedures of behavioral rehearsal, coaching, feedback, modeling, shaping and assignments. Self-report by patients showed that 78% of 50 consecutive interpersonal scenes generalized successfully to the patients' natural milieus. When another set of 50 consecutive scenes were evaluated by direct behavioral observation, 80% generalization was reported.

Laws, D. R., & Serber, M. Measurement and evaluation of Assertive Training with sexual offenders. In R. E. Hosford, & S. Moss (Eds.), *The crumbling walls: Treatment and counseling of the youthful offender.* Champaign, IL.: University of Illinois Press, 1974.

A 24-year-old male pedophile was video taped while being exposed to three simulated variations of a familiar social encounter. A 23-year-old female nurse played the standardized counter-roles. The authors discuss how the target behaviors (verbal dysfluency and body expression) were selected and how this procedure could be used to select and evaluate subsequent training.

Lazarus, A. A. Behavior rehearsal vs. nondirective therapy vs. advice in effecting behavior change. *Behaviour Research and Therapy,* 1966, *4,* 209-212.

The author reports the advantage of behavior rehearsal (modeling plus role playing and feedback) over other methods in helping patients reach their clinical goals. The evaluation of improvement was done anecdotally and there were no controls against the bias of the therapist affecting the results.

Lazarus, A. A. *Behavior therapy and beyond.* New York: McGraw-Hill, 1971.

A transcript of a case interview is presented with Lazarus as therapist. Lazarus points out the utility of a broader definition of interpersonal-emotional skills than the term "assertiveness" permits. Chapter 6, "Acquiring habits of emotional freedom," focuses on the components of assertiveness or personal effectiveness. The book represents a clear, graphic display of the author's rich and extensive clinical experience, but does not report research or experimental results. It is a valuable guide for clinicians.

Liberman, R. P. Behavioral methods in group and family therapy. *Seminars in Psychiatry,* 1972, *4,* 145-156.(a)

The author discusses and cites research to support the therapist's strong influence on group behavior. Structured behavioral methods in directive group therapy are defined as Assertive Training. The uses of Assertive Training with depressed patients and with a range of clients in a community mental health center are described. The advantages of a behavioral approach and its potential impact for further clinical and research progress in group therapies are outlined.

Liberman, R. P. *A guide to behavioral analysis and therapy.* New York: Pergamon Press, 1972.(b)

In Chapter 10, "Behavior therapy with neurotics," the author discusses the goals of Assertive Training, its underlying theory, and the behavioral principles involved. The material is presented in a programmed learning format that provides immediate feedback. The book is divided into two parts. Part I covers the basic principles of behavior and learning, and Part II describes the applications of behavior therapy to a variety of clinical problems and areas. The book can be read in three hours and is particularly appropriate for busy clinicians and professionals who have an interest in gaining a quick but comprehensive overview of behavioral principles and treatment methods.

McFall, R. M., & Lillesand, D. B. Behavioral rehearsal with modeling and coaching in Assertion Training. *Journal of Abnormal Psychology*, 1971, *77*, 313-323.

Nonassertive college students received two sessions of training in refusing unreasonable requests from a solicitor of merchandise. The training consisted of overt and covert response practice, symbolic verbal modeling, and therapist coaching. Compared to no-treatment control subjects, the behavioral rehearsal subjects improved dramatically in their assertive-refusal behavior on self-report and behavioral laboratory measures. Covert rehearsal tended to produce the greatest improvement.

McFall, R. M., & Marston, A. R. An experimental investigation of behavioral rehearsal in Assertive Training. *Journal of Abnormal Psychology*, 1970, *76*, 295-303.

Forty-two college students were assigned to one of the following conditions: (1) behavioral rehearsal with performance feedback (audio tape); (2) behavioral rehearsal without performance feedback; (3) placebo therapy; and (4) no-treatment. Behavioral, self-report, psychophysiological, and *in vivo* tests revealed that the two behavioral rehearsal procedures resulted in significantly greater improvements in assertive performance. Adding performance feedback to behavioral rehearsal did not produce a significant improvement in results.

McFall, R. M., & Twentyman, C. T. Four experiments on the relative contributions of rehearsal, modeling, and coaching to Assertion Training. *Journal of Abnormal Psychology*, 1973, *81*, 199-218.

The training components of rehearsal and coaching both made significant, additive contributions to improved performance in self-report and behavioral assertion measures; however, symbolic modeling added little to the effects of rehearsal alone or rehearsal plus coaching. Positive treatment effects generalized from trained to untrained situations and from laboratory to real-life situations.

Miller, P. M., Hersen, M., Eisler, R. M., & Hilsman, G. Effects of social stress on operant drinking of alcoholics and social drinkers. *Behaviour Research and Therapy*, 1974, *12*, 67-72.

This study demonstrates a relationship between social stress and excessive drinking in alcoholics. After being confronted with standardized, simulated social situations necessitating assertive behavioral responses, alcoholics would increase their rates of lever pressing responses to obtain alcohol on an operant task and showed increases in autonomic reactivity.

Nelson, R., Gibson, F., & Cutting, D. S. Videotaped modeling: The development of three appropriate responses in a mildly retarded child. *Mental Retardation*, 1973, *11*, 24-28.

A modified multiple baseline procedure using modeling, instructions plus social reinforcement, and modeling plus instructions plus social reinforcement was used to increase social responses of a seven-year-old, mildly retarded boy. The superiority of the last procedure is discussed together with the advantages of using nonretarded peers as models, and video tape for presenting models.

Neuman, D. R. Using Assertive Training. In J. D. Krumboltz, & C. E. Thoresen (Eds.), *Behavioral counseling: Cases and techniques.* New York: Holt, Rinehart and Winston, 1969.

This chapter presents a case study of a young man who was successfully coached to increase his dating and peer relationships. Peer modeling, behavioral rehearsal, and journal-keeping were employed. Parts of therapy transcripts are included.

Patterson, R. Time-Out and Assertive Training for a dependent child. *Behavior Therapy*, 1972, *3*, 466-468.

A case study is reported of a nine-year-old boy referred because of frequent crying. The utility of time-out to reduce the frequency of crying was reported, and also the necessity for Assertive Training to develop the boy's ability to defend his rights. A wrestling role play was successful in teaching him to be appropriately assertive, and these gains were reported to generalize in the home.

Rathus, S. A. An experimental investigation of Assertive Training in a group setting. *Journal of Behavior Therapy and Experimental Psychiatry*, 1972, *3*, 81-86.

Fifty-seven women college students were randomly assigned to one of three groups: Assertive Training, discussion, and no treatment. Groups of six students met for seven weekly sessions. In the assertive groups, the students practiced the following exercises in role playing and in "homework" assignments: assertive talk, feeling talk, greetings, disagreeing, asking why, talking about oneself, avoiding justifying opinions, looking people in the eye. The members of the discussion groups met to discuss fears and other interpersonal matters. The students in the Assertive Training groups showed statistically significant increases in self-reported and directly observed assertiveness and greater fear reduction than the no-treatment group. Differences between the Assertive Training group and the discussion group favored the former but not at a statistically significant level.

Rathus, S. A. A 30-item schedule for assessing assertive behavior. *Behavior Therapy*, 1973, *4*, 398-406.

A 30-item schedule for measuring assertiveness is presented, which has moderate to high test-retest reliability and split-half reliability. Satisfactory validity in terms of the impressions respondents make on other people and their indications of how they would behave in specific situations is reported. Item analysis, use of a shorter version, and the issue that assertiveness covaries negatively with impressions of respondents' "niceness" are discussed.

Rimm, D. C., & Masters, J. C. *Behavior Therapy: Techniques and empirical findings.* New York: Academic Press, 1974.

This book is one of the most comprehensive and up-to-date reviews of the entire field of behavior therapy. The use of Assertion Training is described together with much of the relevant research literature up to 1972. For the reader interested in an exhaustive academic introduction to the field of behavior therapy, this book is necessary reading.

Salter, A. *Conditioned reflex therapy.* New York: Farrar, Straus, 1949.

One of the first clinicians to use and write about therapy which focused directly on the patient's behavior, Salter popularized the technique known as Assertion Training. The sections of the book which describe the encouragement of assertiveness in clients has rich clinical value as well as historical interest.

166

Serber, M. Teaching the nonverbal components of Assertive Training. *Journal of Behavior Therapy and Experimental Psychiatry,* 1972, *3,* 1-5.

The author, a pioneer in the application of Assertive Training, describes the behavioral components of assertiveness which can be systematically taught. These include eye contact, use of hands, and gestures, facial expression, posture, voice loudness/tone, and speech fluency.

Serber, M., & Nelson, P. The ineffectiveness of systematic desensitization and Assertive Training in hospitalized schizophrenics. *Journal of Behavior Therapy and Experimental Psychiatry,* 1971, *2,* 107-109.

Desensitization or Assertive Training or both were applied to 24 hospitalized schizophrenics who displayed phobias, lack of interpersonal assertiveness, or both. They received up to 18 treatment sessions. In none of the patients did desensitization produce any reduction of avoidance of the feared objects. The Assertive Training (using modeling and behavior rehearsal), produced minimal improvement in two patients that was maintained at a six-month follow-up.

Shoemaker, M. E., & Paulson, T. L. Group Assertive Training for mothers: A family intervention strategy. Unpublished manuscript. Available from the authors at Development Center, Fuller Graduate School of Psychology; 190 North Oakland Ave., Pasadena, CA.

This study is concerned with a family intervention strategy focusing on the importance of mother's behavior, yet also assessing the husband's verbal responses and the behavior of the original problem child. After training in assertion and communication, mothers exhibited significant increases in assertive responses and decreases in aggressive responses. Husbands' and childrens' behavior also improved. Self-report measures and vignettes were employed for evaluation.

Wallace, C. J., Teigen, J. R., Liberman, R. P., & Baker, V. Destructive behavior treated by contingency contracts and Assertive Training: A case study. *Journal of Behavior Therapy and Experimental Psychiatry,* 1973, *4,* 273-274.

This is a case report of the use of Assertive Training and contingency contracting to reduce violently aggressive behavior in a handicapped

22-year-old male. Assertive Training spanned 25 scenes in four hierarchies of appropriate verbal behavior, each scene role played a minimum of 2 times. The contingency contract specified that home visits would be contingent upon no assaultive behavior in the previous seven days. Results indicated only one instance of assaultive behavior during the 37 days of treatment, and only one instance of aggressive behavior during a 9-month followup.

Weathers, L., & Liberman, R. P. The Porta-Prompter: A new electronic prompting and feedback device. *Behavior Therapy*, 1973, *4*, 703-705.

The Porta-Prompter consists of a sound-shielded microphone, amplifier, switching circuits and battery pack built into a pint volume polyethylene shell. Four miniature earphones can be used by a therapist or trainer to communicate with up to four clients or students. Prompts and verbal feedback can be given to guide subjects' performance without interfering with ongoing interaction. The Porta-Prompter can be used to teach social skills in family therapy, group Assertion Training, and in professional training programs.

Weinman, B., Gelbart, P., Wallace, M., & Post, M. Inducing assertive behavior in chronic schizophrenics: A comparison of socioenvironmental, desensitization, and relaxation therapies. *Journal of Consulting and Clinical Psychology*, 1972, *39*, 246-252.

Socioenvironmental treatment, systematic desensitization, and relaxation training were compared for effectiveness in inducing assertive behavior and decreasing self-reported anxiety. Results showed that socioenvironmental treatment was more effective with older male schizophrenics and systematic desensitization and relaxation training with younger male schizophrenics in generating assertive behavior. There were no other differential treatment effects, although all conditions did generate a decrease in anxiety.

Wolpe, J. *The practice of behavior therapy.* New York: Pergamon Press, 1974.

Wolpe, who helped to develop the term "Assertive Training," describes the technique as a means of overcoming, through counterconditioning, anxiety responses and inhibitions. As one of the "fathers" of behavior therapy, Wolpe provides a description of Assertion Training and other techniques in the context of his theoretical assumptions regarding the learning and unlearning of neurotic habits through "reciprocal inhibition."

Wolpe, J., & Lazarus, A. A. *Behavior therapy techniques.* New York: Pergamon Press, 1966.

Two of the pioneers of behavior therapy collaborated on this manual for clinicians. Systematic desensitization as well as Assertion Training is covered with many case examples. An assertiveness inventory is provided in the Appendix. Unfortunately, this book is out of print. It has been superceded by the authors' newer texts.

Wolpe, J. *Psychotherapy by reciprocal inhibition.* Stanford, CA.: Stanford University Press, 1958.

This book, by the inventor of the systematic desensitization method, gives the theoretical formulation for this treatment procedure. Dr. Wolpe also applies the concept of reciprocal inhibition to assertive behaviors, giving his explanation of assertive behavior as a means of overcoming anxiety and fear.